TASTEFUL TENNIS
Team Tennis Cuisine and Counsel

by

Jane Finkbeiner

and

Martha Williamson

Illustrated by
Kathy Heath

BOLDER BOOKS
Maitland, FL

1

ISBN: 0-9627221-0-3

Library of Congress Catalog
Card Number **90-082933**

Copyright © 1990 by
Jane Finkbeiner and *Martha Williamson*

Published by
BOLDER BOOKS
1660 Indian Dance Court
Maitland, FL 32751

Printed in the United States of America
by Vaughan Press
Orlando, FL

DEDICATION

To the magic of women's team tennis. It transforms athletes into team players and team players into athletes.

Table of Contents

ACKNOWLEDGEMENTS

Thank you for helping us

to our husbands for their congenial contributions,

to Kathy Heath, artist and team tennis player, for capturing our vision on paper,

to the women's team tennis players who took time away from the courts to contribute their special recipes,

to the women's team tennis players of Central Florida who shared their original ideas on entertaining and team management,

to Carolyn Planck, encouraging teacher and friend.

Thank you for inspiring us

to our tennis pros and coaches who cared enough to tell us the truth and encouraged us to become better than we ever believed we could be,

to Col. Nick Powel, author of *The Code* — a man who understood that real kindness is based on fairness and absolute integrity,

to Billie Jean King, women's team tennis pioneer, for showing us what a real champion is made of.

PREFACE

Women's team tennis has been such a wonderful experience for us that we want to share it with everyone. We used our experiences with cooking, team tennis, therapy and books to produce *Tasteful Tennis*. Our book displays the best features of team tennis (fun and food) and helps you avoid the worst feature of team tennis (mental anguish). In these pages we share our recipes, our party ideas, our organizational knowledge and our relationship skills with you.

We have played on a tennis team for nine years now. That's how we first met. Through team tennis we made other lasting friendships on our team and in various leagues. We discovered that strangers across our country who meet and reveal they play team tennis share an instant rapport.

When we joined a team we had vague ideas of improving our tennis somehow. What we got was a lot more than that. We certainly did improve our skills. Starting as beginners, we've risen to above average status. Our team advanced several levels.

Through team tennis we also learned valuable management skills such as planning, negotiating, leading meetings, records keeping, and getting along with people in groups. These skills have been very useful in our homes, work and social lives.

Fortunately we already knew how to have fun. Our team gave us a reason every week to have it. Some of our most traumatic moments on the tennis court evolved into the funniest stories later. We've had terrific parties and memorable lunches together. Amateur team players are not usually motivated solely by athletic ambition. We love getting together with our teammates to exchange ideas, food, information, emotional support, laughs, recipes and also solve problems.

Becoming part of a tennis team involves becoming part of other people's lives. We have all shared our troubles, our joys, our know-how and our anger with each other. We worked together to meet our team goals, which were to improve our tennis and to have fun. Each member knows she made a valuable contribution. There is a special bond among all of us who have ever been on our team because of this sense of common purpose.

Both of us became involved in our local team tennis scene at the league level too. We have been captains, co-captains and served on league boards. Jane is the former Director of the Maitland (Florida) Public Library. She wrote an earlier cookbook called *Roses Are Red, Tennis Balls Are Yellow. This Team Cooks Fancy Stuff Like Strawberry Jello.* Martha is a retired marriage and family therapist. She teaches journal writing workshops now. Our book has two sections—*Cuisine* (the cookbook) and *Counsel* (the handbook).

Cuisine

Gladys Heldman wrote a hilarious foreword to a tennis cookbook years ago. She graphically described the disasters which ensue when tennis players try to cook without specific guidance. The usual problem is lack of time. We need two different kinds of recipes, one kind for entertaining and another for the required daily dinner.

For entertaining we emphasize make ahead and deceptively simple recipes. Over the years we noticed that every time certain dishes were served, everyone asked for the recipes. We collected a number of those winners for your use. *Cuisine* includes a big section exclusively devoted to tennis entertaining.

The key to producing delicious daily dinners is to use very easy, fast recipes. Many of these recipes were kept secret until now because they aren't served at parties. Here they are for the first time. Numerous team players generously share their own family favorites so that you too can spend more time on the courts and less in the kitchen. Many recipes are the kind you can put together and then leave alone to cook for an hour or more. This cooking period gives you the chance to take a shower, catch up on daily chores or even play a match. Others are less than ½ hour from start to finish for those of us who rush into the kitchen at the last possible moment. All the recipes were contributed by team players.

Counsel

Tasteful Tennis is the first guide to amateur team tennis. Libraries and bookstores are full of tennis magazines and books. They tell you how to play better tennis. They also tell you how tennis stars train and entertain. But they don't tell you a thing about amateur team tennis. Our book is different; it contains no tennis instruction at all. We are not qualified to teach anyone to play tennis. Instead we're giving you information you can't find anywhere else about team play.

Our goal for the handbook section is to provide answers to the same old questions and problems that come up year after year (you know the ones about strength, rotation, matching partners, temper tantrums, etc.). With these problems covered in our book new players and/or captains can focus on playing tennis instead of tearing their hair. You won't need to waste another week trying to figure out how to make a lineup or get along with your teammates. We've learned the hard way what works and what doesn't. This book spells it all out for you.

We emphasize the structure of teams and the personalities on them. That's because those are the most important aspects of teams. This handbook includes specific advice for captains. It covers the broad issues (like what team spirit is) and the trivial ones too (what gifts never to give to tennis players).

Amateur team tennis is sweeping the USA today. Since Billie Jean King promoted the team concept for professionals, amateurs have seized the idea and run away with it. In the greater Orlando area alone, the number of leagues has grown from three to eight, including about 2500 adults. We have leagues for men, women, mixed doubles, seniors, working women and even noncompetitive social play. Of course there are even greater numbers of team players in large urban centers like Atlanta and Dallas/Fort Worth.

Despite the marketing opportunity these numbers represent, the commercial interests have taken very little notice of the amateur player. They still focus on professional tennis players on T.V. and in the two tennis magazines. There is still a great gap in the supply of appealing tennis themed giftware. For the most part, businesses do not underwrite tennis teams as they have done for children's little league teams. All this will surely change in the future. We are becoming more visible. One car maker, for instance, does now sponsor a nationwide league. A few retail stores do give us discounts on team uniforms. There is hope for recognition.

Tennis resources are still not well coordinated throughout the country. Most players still don't know what the United States Tennis Association does, and more specifically, what it can do for them. The U.S.T.A. has great resources, many of which we have listed in our Bibliography. It is also the logical body to coordinate team tennis activities all over the U.S.A. A newcomer to a community should be able to call one local number and be directed to an appropriate league. League membership dues should automatically cover local and national U.S.T.A. membership.

We are excited about participating in the nationwide trend for joining adult teams. *Tasteful Tennis* will help you get the most from your team experience.

INTRODUCTION

Our book is divided into two parts. *Cuisine* comes first. It is the cookbook. *Counsel* is next. It is the handbook.

You'll find over 250 recipes in *Cuisine*. We've also included lowfat suggestions. Tennis parties are a big part of team life. We've gathered some inside secrets for entertainment success to help you have more fun. The Index to Recipes is right after the *Cuisine* section.

Counsel has its own introduction and index.

APPETIZERS

Hot Artichoke Dip
A dependable hors d'oeuvre

1 (14-ounce) can artichoke hearts, drained
1 cup mayonnaise
1 cup Parmesan cheese (freshly grated is best)
2 dashes Tabasco sauce
¼ teaspoon red pepper
Dash of garlic powder, optional

Place all ingredients in a blender or food processor and process for 20 seconds or until smooth. Place in a lightly greased 9-inch square baking dish. Bake at 350°F for 25-30 minutes. Serve hot with assorted crackers, Fritos, or raw vegetables. Serves 8-10.

– Terri Parsons

Hot Beef Dip

1 (8-ounce) carton sour cream
1 (8-ounce) package cream cheese, softened
1 (2½-3½-ounce) jar dried beef, chopped
1 small onion, chopped
1 small green pepper, chopped
1½ tablespoons milk
½ cup chopped pecans

Mix first 6 ingredients together and put in a 1-quart buttered dish. Brown pecans in a pan and sprinkle over the top. Bake at 350°F for 30 minutes or until bubbly. Serve with crackers. Serves 16.

– Denise Legan

Crabmeat Dip

1 (8-ounce) package cream cheese, softened
2 tablespoons milk
1 (6½-ounce) can crabmeat
2 tablespoons minced onions
2 tablespoons horseradish
½ teaspoon salt
⅛ teaspoon pepper
Sliced almonds, optional

Preheat oven to 350°F. Mix all ingredients except the almonds and place in a 1-quart baking dish. Add almonds on top if you wish. Bake in preheated oven about 30 minutes or until bubbly. Serve with Triscuits. Makes 8-10 servings.

– Gigi Roberts

Pineapple Cheese Ball
The flavor of Hawaii

2 (8-ounce) packages cream
cheese, softened
1 (8½-ounce) can crushed
pineapple, drained
⅓ cup chopped pecans
¼ cup chopped green pepper
2 tablespoons chopped green
onion
1 tablespoon Lawry's Seasoned
Salt
1 cup chopped nuts to coat cheese
ball

Place cream cheese in bowl; stir
in pineapple, ⅓ cup pecans, pepper,
onion and salt. Cover and chill for
several hours. Make a ball of the
mixture and roll in 1 cup of chopped
nuts. Serve with Pepperidge Farm
Butter Thins. Serves 12-16.

NOTE: Use only "Lawry's Seasoned
Salt" - it makes this cheese ball
unique.

– Ruth Darwin
Penny Edson
Patty Jones
Cairn Ustler

Crab or Shrimp Mold

1 (8-ounce) package cream cheese
1 (10¾-ounce) can tomato soup
2 packages unflavored gelatin
½ cup cold water
¾ cup mayonnaise
1½ cups canned crabmeat,
drained and dried, *or* fresh
crabmeat or fresh shrimp,
cooked, shelled and chopped
to measure 1½ cups
1 cup minced celery
½ cup chopped green pepper
1 or 2 green onions, minced
½ teaspoon sugar

Place cream cheese and tomato
soup in a large saucepan and heat
just until cheese is melted. Dissolve
gelatin in cold water. Combine the
soup/cheese mixture with the gelatin and mix these with all other ingredients. Pour into a 3½ or 4-quart
mold and chill for 2 to 3 hours. Unmold and serve with crackers.
Serves approximately 24 as an
appetizer.

– Becky Dunn

Crab Mold

1 envelope unflavored gelatin
3 tablespoons cold water
1 (10¾-ounce) can cream of
  mushroom soup
1 (8-ounce) package cream cheese
1 cup mayonnaise
1 cup celery, finely chopped
1 cup onion, finely chopped
2 (6-ounce) cans crab or
  1 (8-ounce) package frozen
  fresh crabmeat

Grease a 6-cup mold or bowl. Dissolve gelatin in water. Heat soup until warm. Remove from heat and add gelatin. Add cream cheese and stir until melted. Mix in remaining ingredients. Put in mold. Chill overnight or at least 8 hours. Serve with crackers. Serves 24.

– Ronee Olson

Chopped Herring Appetizer
Stimulates the appetite

1 pound Vita herring in wine
  sauce
1 large slice challah or ½ Kaiser
  roll
4 hard cooked eggs
1 large tart apple, peeled and
  sliced
For garnish: parsley, chopped egg
  yolk, and/or lemon slices

Drain herring and use the juice to soak bread. Chop herring, soaked bread, eggs and apple together in a food processor until mixed well. Refrigerate until ready for serving. Serve with party rye or pumpernickel bread or crackers. Makes 4-6 servings.

– Tybe Kahn

Hummus
High protein from the Mid East

2 cloves garlic
1 (19-ounce) can garbanzo beans
1 cup olive oil
⅓ cup fresh lemon juice
3 tablespoons Tahini (sesame
  butter)
1 teaspoon salt

Place garlic in a food processor and crush. Add the rest of the ingredients and blend until thick. Serve with pita bread or sliced fresh carrots.

NOTE: Tahini can be found in health food stores. Or you can substitute 3 tablespoons creamy peanut butter and 1 tablespoon sesame oil. Mix well and use in place of the Tahini.

– Joanne Ehrlich

Smoked Salmon Paté

Make ahead gourmet

1 (16-ounce) can salmon, bones
  removed and flaked
1 (8-ounce) package cream cheese
2 tablespoons grated or finely
  chopped onion
1 tablespoon lemon juice
¼ teaspoon pepper or dash of
  Tabasco
1 tablespoon liquid smoke
1 teaspoon prepared horseradish
  (optional)
¼ teaspoon salt
Chopped nuts
Parsley or paprika

Combine the salmon and the next 7 ingredients. Shape into a ball or roll and chill several hours. Decorate with chopped nuts and parsley or paprika. Serve with crackers. Serves about 12.

NOTE: This can be made ahead and kept nicely in the refrigerator for several days.

– Ruth Darwin

Artichoke Squares

Luscious

2 (6-ounce) jars marinated
  artichoke hearts
2 tablespoons butter
1 medium onion, finely chopped
1 garlic clove, minced
4 eggs, beaten
¼ cup fine bread crumbs
¼ teaspoon salt
⅛ teaspoon pepper
⅛ teaspoon oregano
⅛ teaspoon Tabasco sauce
2 cups shredded sharp Cheddar
  cheese
2 tablespoons minced parsley

Preheat oven to 350°F. Drain artichoke hearts and discard marinade (or use it to make your favorite salad dressing). Chop artichoke hearts and set aside. Heat butter. Add onion and garlic and sauté until onion is tender. Combine eggs, bread crumbs, salt, pepper, oregano, and Tabasco sauce. Fold in cheese and parsley. Add chopped artichoke hearts and sautéed onion mixture, blending well. Pour into a 9-inch square glass baking dish. Bake in preheated oven for about 30 minutes. Cool briefly before cutting into 1-inch squares. The artichoke squares may also be served cold. May be prepared and cooked a day or two ahead and reheated in a 350°F oven for 10-12 minutes.

– Gigi Roberts

Cheesy Artichoke Heart Appetizers

2 (8-ounce) cans refrigerated
  crescent dinner rolls
¾ cup (3 ounces) shredded
  mozzarella cheese
1 (3-ounce) can (¾ cup) grated
  Parmesan cheese
½ cup salad dressing
1 (14-ounce) can artichoke hearts,
  drained and finely chopped
1 (4-ounce) can chopped green
  chilies, drained (optional)

Unroll dinner roll dough into rectangles; press together onto bottom and sides of a 15x10x1-inch jelly roll pan to form crust. Bake at 375°F for 10 minutes.

Meanwhile, combine the remaining ingredients and mix well. Spread over the crust after it has baked for 10 minutes. Bake for another 15 minutes or until the cheese is melted. Let stand for 5 minutes before serving. Cut into squares and garnish with thin red pepper strips. Makes approximately 3 dozen appetizers.

– Gail Loeffler

Mushroom Cheese Appetizers
Freezes beautifully

2 cups baking mix
½ cup cold water
¼ pound bulk pork sausage
¼ cup chopped green onion
¾ cup mayonnaise
1 pound fresh mushroom caps
2 cups shredded Cheddar cheese
  (8 ounces)
Paprika

Heat oven to 350°F. Grease a 13x9x2-inch pan. Mix baking mix and water until soft dough forms; then beat 20 strokes. Press into the pan. Cook sausage in skillet and drain. Mix sausage with onion, mayonnaise and the stems only of the mushrooms. Fill the mushroom caps with the sausage mixture. Place stuffed mushrooms in a row on the dough in the pan; sprinkle with cheese and paprika. Cover pan loosely with aluminum foil. Bake for 20 minutes; remove foil. Bake another 5-10 minutes until the cheese is bubbly. Let stand for 15 minutes and then cut into pieces. Makes 25 appetizers.

– Nanci A. Bilanski

Stuffed Mushrooms

¾ pound bacon
1 pound mushrooms
1 teaspoon fresh minced garlic
2 tablespoons butter
½ teaspoon salt
¼ teaspoon pepper
8 ounces shredded sharp Cheddar
  cheese

Fry bacon until crisp; crumble. Pull stems from mushrooms. Chop stems and sauté in butter until soft. Add salt and pepper. Fold in cheese and bacon. Over-stuff each mushroom cap with the mushroom/cheese/bacon mixture. Bake at 350°F for 20 minutes. Makes about 20 appetizers.

– Gigi Roberts

Cheese Olive Pupu
Treasured treat

1 cup mayonnaise
1 cup shredded sharp Cheddar
  cheese
½ cup chopped ripe olives (more
  to taste if desired)
½ cup chopped green onion
½ teaspoon salt
½ teaspoon pepper
½ teaspoon curry powder
6 English muffins, halved

Mix first 7 ingredients. Spread mixture on each muffin half. Cut the muffin halves into quarters and bake at 350°F for 10 minutes. If you wish you may freeze the Pupus by placing them on a cookie sheet and freezing; when frozen place in plastic bag to store. To serve, thaw, wrap in foil, and reheat in a 300°F oven for 10-15 minutes. Makes 48 appetizers.

NOTE: Pupu means treasure in Chinese.

– Denise Legan

Cheese Snack Rounds

1 (5-ounce) jar sharp pasteurized
process cheese spread
½ cup baking mix
2 tablespoons toasted sesame
seeds

Mix cheese spread and baking mix. On a lightly floured pastry cloth or covered board, shape mixture into a roll about 1-inch in diameter. Roll in sesame seed, pressing seed in lightly if necessary. Wrap and refrigerate until firm, at least 2 hours.

Heat oven to 375°F. Cut roll into ¼-inch slices. Place on a lightly greased cookie sheet. Bake until golden brown, 8-10 minutes. Makes about 42 appetizers.

– Ginny Milks

Bacon Stix

Easy make ahead treat

10 thin bread sticks - any flavor
5 slices bacon cut in half
lengthwise
½ cup grated Parmesan cheese

Dredge one side of bacon strips in cheese. Roll 1 bacon strip diagonally around each bread stick. Place sticks on microwave baking sheet lined with paper towels. Microwave on high 4½-6 minutes. Roll again in cheese. Serve warm or at room temperature. Serves 10.

NOTE: Stix can be made ahead and held in refrigerator. When ready to serve, microwave as directed. They can also be cooked ahead and held for several hours before being served at room temperature.

– Betsy Hemphill

Dipped Chips

1 (12½-ounce) package tortilla
  chips
¼ to ½ (8-ounce) bottle ranch
  salad dressing
1 to 2 bunches scallions, chopped
1½ cups Cheddar cheese

Cover the bottom of a 13x9-inch pan with tortilla chips (the whole package may not be needed). Spread ranch dressing to taste over the top of the chips. Sprinkle chopped scallions to taste over the dressing. Cover all with cheese. Bake at 350°F for 10-15 minutes. Serve immediately.

– Kathy Cook

Hot Sausage Balls in Sour Cream
Intriguing

2 pounds highly seasoned bulk
  sausage
1 (8-ounce) jar Major Grey's
  Chutney
1 cup sherry
1 cup sour cream

Roll sausage into bite-size balls; cook in skillet until lightly browned. Pour off grease and remove balls to chafing dish. Put chutney in skillet; add sherry and sour cream. Cook gently and pour over sausage balls.

NOTE: Yogurt can be substituted for the sour cream.

– Carolyn Nelson

Marinated Chicken Wings

3 to 5 garlic cloves, crushed
1 cup soy sauce
1 cup orange marmalade
1 teaspoon black pepper
1 teaspoon ginger
15 to 25 chicken wings cut in half,
  wing tips discarded

Mix together all ingredients except the chicken wings. Place the chicken wings in a shallow baking pan and cover with marinade. Cover the pan and chill the marinated chicken wings 8 hours or overnight. Bake, uncovered, at 300°F for 45 minutes or until tender. Makes 15-25 wings.

– Nancy Juarez

Oriental Chicken Wings

Tastes like you've slaved for hours

1 cup soy sauce
1 cup brown sugar
¼ cup butter
¼ cup Sauterne
1 teaspoon dry mustard
2 pounds chicken wings

Mix all ingredients, except chicken wings, together and heat in saucepan until the butter is melted. Pour the marinade over the chicken wings and marinate overnight. Place chicken and marinade in a shallow pan and cook at 350°F for about 1 hour or until the meat is tender. Drain the marinade and continue baking the wings for about 15 minutes to make them crispy. Serves 4-6.

NOTE: Don't try to reheat - wings will get too sticky.

– Colleen Aboud

Appetizer Pie

Unique

1 frozen (9-inch) pastry shell, thawed (or make your own)
12 ounces cream cheese
2 ounces bleu cheese
½ cup mayonnaise
½ teaspoon onion or garlic salt
Garnishes: cherry tomato halves, sliced mushrooms, chopped parsley, chopped hard cooked eggs, sliced ripe olives

On a large baking sheet, pat pastry into an 11-inch circle; pierce thoroughly with fork. Bake pastry for 8 minutes at 425°F or until lightly browned. Cool. Place pastry on serving platter. Beat next 4 ingredients until fluffy; spread evenly on pastry. Cover; chill at least 4 hours. Just before serving, garnish in circles, starting with tomatoes and ending with olives. Makes 12 (2½-inch) wedges.

– Marge Nagle

Vegetable Pizza
Eye appealing

2 (8-ounce) packages crescent rolls
1 (16-ounce) package cream cheese
⅔ cup mayonnaise
1 (1-ounce) package dry ranch salad dressing mix
Choice of raw vegetables: broccoli flowerets; cauliflower flowerets; sliced fresh mushrooms; sliced black and/or green olives; sliced radishes; sliced carrots
1 (4-ounce) package shredded Cheddar cheese

Press crescent rolls on the bottom and up the sides of a 10x15-inch jelly roll pan. Bake at 375°F for 14 minutes; cool. Beat together cream cheese, mayonnaise and Hidden Valley Ranch Dressing. Spread on the cooled crust. Place chosen vegetables on the cream cheese in a decorative pattern. Sprinkle with Cheddar cheese. Cut into 24 squares. Refrigerate and serve cold. Makes 24 hors d'oeuvres.

– Donna Swenson

Marinated Broccoli Hors D'oeuvre
A real crowd pleaser

3 bunches fresh broccoli
1 cup cider vinegar
1 tablespoon sugar
1 tablespoon dill weed
1 tablespoon Accent
1 teaspoon salt
1 teaspoon pepper
1 teaspoon fresh minced garlic
1½ cups vegetable oil

Cut broccoli into small flowerets and reserve the rest for use in your favorite vegetable soup, casserole, etc. Mix remaining ingredients. Pour dressing over broccoli flowerets. Cover and refrigerate for 24 hours. (You may marinate in a large plastic bag.) Baste frequently. Drain and serve. Serves 12-14.

NOTE: This hors d'oeuvre is easy to transport to parties if you marinate it in a one-gallon plastic bag. Leftover dressing is great on any green salad.

– Gigi Roberts

Garden Medley

Appetizer or salad

2 tomatoes, peeled
1 cucumber
1 small onion
1 bell pepper
1 cup celery
1 package unflavored gelatin
½ cup cold water
½ cup boiling water
1 cup lowfat cottage cheese
1 cup lo-cal, no-cholesterol
  mayonnaise
½ teaspoon salt

Chop tomatoes, cucumber, onion, bell pepper and celery finely and drain on a paper towel. Dissolve unflavored gelatin in cold water; add boiling water. In a blender or food processor, cream cottage cheese; blend with mayonnaise and salt. Blend in gelatin and vegetables. Congeal and serve with wheat crackers as an appetizer. As a variation you may add an extra ½ teaspoon salt and congeal in minimolds and serve on a lettuce leaf as a salad. Makes 8-10 servings.

– Connie Cavett

Curried Pecans

A substitute for cocktail peanuts

1 cup whole pecans
1 teaspoon curry powder
½ teaspoon seasoned salt
⅛ teaspoon garlic powder
1 to 2 teaspoons vegetable oil

Spread pecans in a single layer in a shallow baking pan. Toast, uncovered, in a 350°F oven until golden, about 8 minutes. Meanwhile add the curry powder, seasoned salt, and garlic powder to the vegetable oil. When pecans are toasted, remove from oven and drizzle with the seasoned oil. Return to the oven for another 2-3 minutes, stirring often. Remove from oven and let stand, uncovered, about 5 minutes to crisp and cool completely. If not serving immediately, store in an airtight container for up to 1 month. Makes 1 cup.

BREADS

Old Fashioned Apricot Bread
A favorite for generations

1 (6-ounce) package dried
  apricots, chopped
1 cup raisins
1½ cups hot water
2 teaspoons soda
2 eggs
2 cups sugar
2 teaspoons vanilla
3½ cups flour
1 teaspoon salt
1 cup pecans

Combine chopped apricots and raisins and pour the hot water over them; let sit until cool, about 20 minutes. Beat the eggs, sugar and vanilla together; add the fruit mixture and stir until combined. Add the flour, salt and nuts and mix well. Pour batter into 2 9x5x3-inch loaf pans that have been treated with no-stick cooking spray. Bake at 300°F for 1½ hours. Makes 2 loaves.

NOTE: The bread pans can be lined with aluminum foil rather than oil and flour. The loaves will lift right out and can be wrapped in the same foil. An added bonus - no pan cleanup. Try with all your fruit bread recipes.

Holiday Cranberry Bread
Take advantage of this seasonal treat

2 cups flour
¾ cup sugar
1½ teaspoons baking powder
1 teaspoon salt
½ teaspoon soda
½ cup chopped nuts
1 cup fresh or frozen cranberries,
  chopped
1 egg, beaten
¾ cup orange juice
2 tablespoons vegetable oil

Sift the dry ingredients together. Stir in the nuts and cranberries. Add remaining ingredients and blend until thoroughly moistened. Bake in a greased, floured loaf pan at 350°F for 50 minutes. Yield: 1 loaf.

–Susan Scott

Kathy's Date Nut Bread
Almost no-fat

1 cup chopped dates
1½ cups boiling water
1 cup sugar
1 tablespoon shortening
1 egg
1 cup chopped nuts
2¾ cups flour
2 level teaspoons baking soda
Pinch of salt
1 teaspoon vanilla

Put dates in boiling water and let sit until cool. Mix all ingredients together including the water the dates have soaked in. Place in a bread pan and bake at 325°F for 1½ hours. Makes 1 loaf.

NOTE: An excellent, moist fruit bread despite the tiny amount of shortening.

Marsala Date Nut Bread
Gourmet delight

2 eggs
2 cups flour
1 cup sugar
½ cup Marsala (no substitutions)
¼ cup oil
1 tablespoon baking powder
¾ teaspoon salt
½ teaspoon baking soda
1½ cups coarsely chopped dates
1 cup coarsely chopped walnuts

Preheat over to 350°F. Beat the eggs in a large bowl for 30 seconds at medium speed. Add the rest of the ingredients, except the dates and nuts, and beat until well blended. Stir in dates and nuts. Turn into bread pan and bake for 55-60 minutes or until a toothpick comes out clean. Remove from pan and cool. Makes 1 loaf.

Rice Bran Muffins

A nice breakfast muffin

2 cups rice bran
2 cups oats, quick or regular
2 teaspoons baking soda
½ teaspoon salt
½ cup brown sugar or 4 to 5 packs
  sugar substitute
1 cup plain non-fat yogurt
¾ cup unsweetened applesauce
¼ cup water
1 tablespoon canola oil
3 egg whites
1 teaspoon vanilla
Grated zest of 1 orange
1½ cups blueberries (or other fruit)

Preheat oven to 400°F. In a large bowl, mix dry ingredients. In a medium bowl, blend yogurt, applesauce, water, oil, egg whites, and vanilla. Stir in grated zest. Combine liquid ingredients with dry ingredients. Mix thoroughly but don't beat. Stir in blueberries. Fill muffin tins (lined with cupcake liners) ¾ full. Bake for 20-25 minutes. Makes 18 muffins.

– Dian Helgerud

Skillet Corn Bread

Team with chili

1 tablespoon bacon drippings
1 teaspoon salt
1 teaspoon baking powder
1 cup corn meal
½ teaspoon baking soda
1 cup buttermilk
1 egg

Melt bacon drippings in an 8-inch iron skillet in a 450°F oven. Combine salt, baking powder and corn meal; set aside. Add baking soda to buttermilk; beat egg and stir into buttermilk mixture. Stir buttermilk mixture into the cormeal mixture; remove skillet from oven and pour the bacon drippings into the corn bread batter. Return batter to skillet and bake at 350°F for 30 minutes. Serves 4.

– Beth Infantino

No Knead Refrigerator Yeast Rolls
A tasty and convenient time saver

1 package dry yeast
2 cups warm water (105 to 115°F)
6 ounces (1½ sticks) margarine, melted
¼ cup sugar
1 egg, beaten
4 cups self-rising flour

Place yeast in water to soften. Cream margarine and sugar together in a large bowl. Add beaten egg, flour, and yeast mixture. Mix well. Place in an airtight bowl that is twice the capacity of the dough (about 4 quarts). Refrigerate at least 8 hours or up to 4 days. To bake, drop dough by the spoonful into well-greased muffin tins. Bake at 350°F for 20 minutes. Makes 24 rolls.

Beer Bread
Excellent for toasting

3 cups self-rising flour
3 tablespoons sugar
1 (12-ounce) can of beer

Mix all ingredients together. Pour into a greased loaf pan. Bake at 350°F for 40-45 minutes. Yield: 1 loaf

NOTE: Add 1 cup raisins to batter and drizzle with 3 tablespoons melted margarine for *Raisin Beer Bread.*

Beer Muffins
A three ingredient wonder

4 cups Bisquick
2 tablespoons sugar
1 (12-ounce) can or bottle of beer at room temperature

Mix all ingredients together. Fill greased muffin cup ⅔ full. Bake at 400°F for 12-15 minutes. Makes 12-15 muffins.

Cinnamon Cheese Puffs
Fun food

1 (10-ounce) can refrigerated
  biscuits
¼ cup margarine, melted
½ teaspoon vanilla
½ cup sugar
1 teaspoon cinnamon
⅓ teaspoon almond extract
1 (3-ounce) package cream cheese

Separate biscuit dough into 10 pieces. Press each piece into a 3-inch circle and set aside. In a small bowl, combine the melted margarine and vanilla. In another small bowl, combine the sugar, cinnamon, and almond extract. Cut the cream cheese into 10 cubes. Dip each cube in the margarine mixture and then in the cinnamon sugar mixture and place on each circle. Fold the dough over the cheese and seal well, shaping into balls. Dip each ball first in the margarine mixture and then in the cinnamon sugar mixture. Place seam side down in ungreased muffin cups. Bake at 375°F for 12-18 minutes. Store leftovers in the refrigerator. Makes 10 puffs.

– Carol Wood

SALADS AND DRESSINGS

Cranberry Frost

An alternative to cranberry relish or sauce

2 (3-ounce) packages cream
  cheese
2 tablespoons sugar
2 tablespoons mayonnaise
1 (16-ounce) can whole berry
  cranberry sauce
1 (20-ounce) can crushed
  pineapple
½ cup chopped pecans
½ cup heavy whipping cream,
  whipped

Blend cream cheese and sugar together. Stir in mayonnaise and fold in other ingredients. Spoon into cupcake paper for individual servings or into a 6-cup mold or pan. Freeze overnight. Serve with a dab of mayonnaise on the top. Serves 20.

NOTE: The frost can be made in individual molds or in an 8½x8½-inch pan. If using pan, cut into squares for serving.

– Sherry Lorenzen

Cranberry Freeze

Pretty

1 (16-ounce) can whole cranberry
  sauce
1 (8¾-ounce) can crushed
  pineapple, drained
1 cup dairy sour cream
¼ cup sifted confectioners sugar
3 pineapple rings, well drained

In medium bowl, combine cranberry sauce and crushed pineapple. In small bowl, stir together sour cream and sifted confectioners sugar; add to fruit mixture, mixing well. Line a 3-cup refrigerator tray with foil; pour in fruit mixture. Freeze until firm.

Before serving, lift frozen salad and foil from pan; let stand a few minutes. Remove foil. Cut into six wedges. Top each wedge with ½ pineapple ring. Serves 6.

NOTE: Top with frozen whipped dessert topping and serve as a dessert.

– Esther Treese

Fruit Medley

6 cups assorted fruits, either fresh or canned (mixture of apricots, grapes, peaches, pears, and pineapple), cut into bite-size pieces
1 cup orange juice
2 teaspoons lemon juice
3 tablespoons honey
2 teaspoons cornstarch
4 halves cantaloupe
1 (3-ounce) package cream cheese or whipped cream cheese

If using canned fruit, pour off liquid and save for another use. Combine orange and lemon juice, cornstarch and honey. Cook over medium heat until clear and thickened, stirring occasionally. Cool slightly. Mix sauce and assorted fruits together. Arrange fruit in melon halves. Whip plain cream cheese with just enough milk to make it whipping consistency, or use whipped cream cheese. Spoon over fruit. Serves 4.

– Tommie Haskins

Frozen Fruit Salad
Lo-cal version of a Southern favorite

1 (8-ounce) package Neufchatel cheese
½ cup mayonnaise
½ cup nonfat plain yogurt
¼ cup sugar (or equivalent sugar substitute)
¼ teaspoon salt
1 (16-ounce) can dark sweet cherries, drained
1 (8¾-ounce) can crushed pineapple, drained
1 (11-ounce) can mandarin oranges, drained
2 cups mini marshmallows
½ cup chopped pecans
1 sliced banana

Beat Neufchatel cheese with electric mixer until fluffy. Add mayonnaise, yogurt, sugar, and salt. Blend. Fold in remaining ingredients. Pour into a loafpan lined with plastic wrap. Freeze at least 6 hours. Let stand 30-45 minutes before serving. Slice and serve. Serves 10-14 depending on size of the slices.

NOTE: Although this is called a salad and is served on lettuce at ladies' luncheons, it is also delicious to eat as a dessert.

Lemon Gelatin Salad

2 (3-ounce) packages lemon
gelatin
1 cup boiling water
1 (16-ounce) container farm style
cottage cheese
1 (20-ounce) can crushed
pineapple, drained
4 stalks celery, chopped fine
1 cup evaporated milk
1½ cups mayonnaise
1 unpeeled apple, chopped fine
1 cup chopped nuts

Dissolve gelatin in the boiling
water. Add the next 7 ingredients in
order, mixing well after each addition. Pour into a 6-cup mold and
refrigerate. Makes 6-8 servings.

– Lynne Wendt

Pistachio Nut Salad

Children love as a salad or dessert

1 (20-ounce) can crushed
pineapple, undrained
1 (3½-ounce) package instant
pistachio pudding & pie filling
1 (8-ounce) carton frozen whipped
dessert topping

Blend pineapple and juice with
pudding mix until well dissolved.
Fold in frozen whipped dessert topping. Pour into a 1-quart serving
dish or bowl. Chill until set. Serves
6-8.

– Betsy Hemphill

Raspberry Applesauce Delight

Also a successful dessert

1 (6-ounce) package raspberry
gelatin
2 cups boiling water
2 cups applesauce

Mix gelatin and water. Add applesauce and mix well. Pour into a
6-cup mold. Chill until firm. Serves
6-8.

– Susan Scott

Watergate Salad

1 (3½-ounce) package instant pistachio pudding
1 (20-ounce) can crushed pineapple, undrained
1 (8-ounce) container frozen whipped dessert topping, thawed
1 (8-ounce) carton sour cream
1 cup mini marshmallows

Mix all ingredients together and place in a 4-6 cup bowl or mold. Chill. Serves 6-8.

– Ellen Koenig

Strawberry Salad

2 (3-ounce) packages strawberry gelatin
1 cup boiling water
2 (10-ounce) packages frozen, sliced strawberries, thawed
1 (20-ounce) can crushed pineapple, drained
3 medium bananas, mashed
1 cup chopped nuts
1 pint sour cream

Combine gelatin with boiling water. Fold in, all at once, strawberries and juice, pineapple, bananas and nuts. Turn ½ of mixture into 12x8x2-inch casserole dish. Chill until firm, about 1½ hours. Evenly spread top with sour cream and gently spoon on rest of mixture. Chill until set. Serves 10-12.

NOTE: To reduce fat and calories, substitute yogurt for sour cream and gelatin with nutrasweet for regular gelatin. This salad also can be served as a dessert.

– Bobii Earle

Tart Melon Salad

Wonderful for brunches and luncheons

3 cups assorted melon balls
1 cup strawberry halves
1 (15-ounce) can unsweetened
   pineapple chunks, drained
1 (11-ounce) can mandarin orange
   segments, drained
1 (6-ounce) can frozen lemonade
   concentrate, thawed and
   undiluted
¼ cup orange marmalade
2 tablespoons Triple Sec
Mint leaves, optional

Place prepared fruit in pretty glass salad bowl. In separate bowl, mix together the lemonade concentrate, orange marmalade and Triple Sec. Pour over fruit and toss gently. Chill in refrigerator at least one hour before serving. Garnish with mint leaves. Serves 6-8.

NOTE: This beautiful and tasty salad can be made up to 5 hours ahead. It has a lovely sweet/tart flavor.

– Becky Dunn

Watermelon and Onion Salad

Refreshing combo

4 cups bite-size watermelon
   chunks or balls
1 small white or Bermuda onion,
   thinly sliced
1 (11-ounce) can mandarin
   oranges, drained
1 (8-ounce) can pineapple chunks,
   drained
2 tablespoons sugar
2 tablespoons vinegar

Mix the watermelon, onion, oranges and pineapple together. Add the sugar to the vinegar and stir until the sugar is dissolved. Drizzle over the fruit. Chill and enjoy. Serves 4.

– Nancy Juarez

Artichoke Salad

1 (4-ounce) jar chopped pimiento,
  drained
1 (8½-ounce) can artichoke hearts,
  drained
1½ cups sliced celery
1 medium onion, thinly sliced
1¼ cups tarragon vinegar
1½ teaspoons Accent or
  monosodium glutamate
1¼ teaspoon salt
1 teaspoon sugar
1 teaspoon fines herbes
¼ teaspoon Tabasco
¼ cup salad oil
¼ cup chopped parsley
2 tablespoons capers

Combine pimiento, artichoke hearts, celery, and onion. Measure vinegar into a blender; add Accent, salt and sugar and blend. Add fines herbes, Tabasco, and salad oil and continue processing until well blended. Pour dressing over the vegetables and refrigerate several hours or overnight. To serve, sprinkle with chopped parsley and capers. Serves 6.

– Sue Steward

Molded Asparagus Salad

2 (14½-ounce) cans asparagus
  pieces
1 cup sugar
Juice of ½ lemon
½ teaspoon salt
2 envelopes unflavored gelatin
½ cup white vinegar
1 cup chopped celery
¾ cup chopped pecans
1 (4-ounce) jar chopped pimientos,
  drained
1 small onion, finely chopped
1 (8-ounce) can sliced water
  chestnuts, drained
½ cup mayonnaise
½ cup sour cream

Drain asparagus, reserving liquid. Add water to asparagus liquid to equal 1 cup. Combine the asparagus liquid, sugar, lemon juice, and salt and bring to a boil. Soften the gelatin in vinegar and stir into the hot asparagus liquid/lemon juice mixture to dissolve. Add asparagus and next 5 ingredients. Mix well and pour into an oiled 6-cup mold. Chill until set. Serve with a dressing made by mixing the mayonnaise and sour cream together. Serves 8.

– Nan Lasbury

Asparagus Salad with Tarragon Marinade
Surprise ingredient - hearts of palm

Salad
1 pound fresh asparagus
1 (16-ounce) can hearts of palm, drained
1 (7-ounce) jar artichoke hearts, rinsed and drained
¾ cup ripe olives
3 tablespoons chopped onion
1 (2-ounce) jar diced pimiento

Marinade
½ cup vegetable oil
2¼ tablespoons tarragon vinegar
1 teaspoon salt
1 teaspoon dry mustard
¼ teaspoon white pepper

Bibb lettuce
2 hard cooked eggs, sliced (optional)

Cook asparagus until tender and drain. Layer vegetables in shallow dish. Combine ingredients for marinade in small jar and shake well. Pour marinade over vegetables. Cover and chill several hours or overnight. Arrange lettuce on platter and top with marinated vegetables. Garnish with sliced hard cooked eggs if desired. Makes 6-8 servings.

NOTE: If you are fond of hearts of palm you can use 2 cans.

– Debora Lindsay

Overnight Salad
Variation of a classic

1 head lettuce, cut up
1 head cauliflower, cut up
1 pound bacon, fried, drained and broken into bits
⅓ cup Parmesan cheese
¼ cup sugar
1 onion, sliced *thinly*
1 pint mayonnaise

Layer each ingredient, in order given, in a 12x9-inch casserole dish. Cover and chill overnight. Toss before serving. Serves 10-12.

– Kathy Reynolds

Caesar Salad
No-fail

⅓ cup olive or vegetable oil
⅓ cup grated Parmesan cheese
2 tablespoons lemon juice
¼ teaspoon salt
⅛ teaspoon cracked or ground
  pepper
1 egg
2 medium heads of romaine or
  leaf lettuce torn into small
  pieces
1 (2-ounce) can anchovies,
  chopped fine
Garlic croutons

Make salad dressing by combining first 6 ingredients in a blender and mixing well. Put lettuce, anchovies, and croutons in salad bowl. Pour dressing over salad. Serves 6.

– Terri Parsons

Bibb and Orange Salad
Serve with roasted Rock Cornish hens

Dressing
½ cup salad oil
¼ cup sugar
¼ cup tarragon vinegar
1 teaspoon dry mustard
1 teaspoon salt
Pepper to taste
½ teaspoon Worcestershire sauce
2 teaspoons minced parsley
1 red onion, thinly sliced

Salad
4 heads Bibb lettuce or Boston
  lettuce
1 bunch watercress
2 (11-ounce) cans mandarin
  oranges, drained
½ cup slivered almonds, toasted

Combine all dressing ingredients and refrigerate for at least 2 hours.

To make salad: wash and dry lettuce and watercress. Just before serving, shake dressing to mix well and pour over lettuce and watercress. Toss oranges and almonds with the greens. Serve immediately. Serves 8-10.

NOTE: Try this dressing on other green salads.

– Carolyn Nelson

Spinach Salad

1 (10-ounce) package fresh
   spinach, washed
1 (4-ounce) can sliced water
   chestnuts
3 hard boiled eggs, diced
3 strips bacon, fried crisply and
   crumbled
1 small onion, thinly sliced

Dressing

1 cup corn oil
¾ cup sugar
⅓ cup catsup
¼ cup wine vinegar
1 tablespoon Worcestershire
   according to taste

Place all salad ingredients in a salad bowl. Beat dressing ingredients together until the sugar dissolves. Pour over the salad. Serves 4.

– Terri Parsons

Spinach Salad with Chutney Dressing
Savory

Dressing

¼ cup wine vinegar
3 tablespoons chutney
1 clove garlic, minced
1 tablespoon prepared mustard
2 teaspoons sugar
¼ cup vegetable oil
Salt and pepper to taste

Salad

1 pound fresh spinach, washed
   and torn into bite-size pieces
6 mushrooms, sliced
1 (8-ounce) can sliced water
   chestnuts, drained
6 slices bacon, cooked and
   crumbled
¼ cup bean sprouts
¼ cup Gruyere cheese
¼ cup thinly sliced red onion

Combine all dressing ingredients in a blender or food processor. Blend on high speed. Combine all salad ingredients. Just before serving, toss the salad with the chutney dressing. Serves 4 as a main course or 6 as a side salad.

– Edie Fagan

Wilted Spinach Salad
The best you'll ever put into your mouth

2 (10-ounce) bags fresh spinach, washed and torn into bite-size pieces
8 slices bacon, crisply fried and crumbled (save bacon drippings)
1 small onion, chopped
¼ cup bacon drippings
½ cup vinegar
½ cup sugar
½ cup water
Dash salt

Put spinach in salad bowl. Sprinkle crumbled bacon over spinach. Sauté onion in pan bacon was cooked in. Add ¼ cup bacon drippings, vinegar, sugar, water and salt. Bring dressing to a boil. Pour immediately over the spinach salad. Serves 4-6.

NOTE: For best results the dressing must be very hot before pouring over spinach.

– Susan Scott

Layered Spinach Salad
So simple - just keep layering

1 (10-ounce) bag fresh spinach, washed and torn into bite-size pieces
½ pound bacon, fried crisply and broken into pieces
4 hard-boiled eggs, chopped
1 head lettuce, torn into pieces
Salt and pepper to taste
1 teaspoon sugar
1 box frozen peas, thawed
1 sweet red onion
2 cups mayonnaise
1 cup sour cream
Grated Swiss cheese to cover top

In a 9x13-inch dish, layer all ingredients, in the order given, except the mayonnaise, sour cream and Swiss cheese. Mix together the mayonnaise and sour cream and spread over the layered ingredients. Sprinkle grated Swiss cheese over the top to taste. Let salad stand overnight, covered with foil. Serves 12.

– Terrie Buys

Cauliflower-Broccoli Toss

1 medium head cauliflower
1 medium bunch broccoli
6 to 8 green onions, chopped
1 cup mayonnaise
½ (.04-ounce) package buttermilk
   salad dressing mix
2 tablespoons sugar
2 tablespoons vinegar

Use only flowerets from both the cauliflower and broccoli. Combine cauliflower and broccoli flowerets with the chopped green onion. Mix the remaining ingredients well and pour over the vegetables. Toss gently, cover, and chill overnight. Serves 8-10.

– Lynne Wendt

Chopped Cole Slaw
Tangy accompaniment

1 large head cabbage, shredded
1 large green pepper, chopped
1 large white onion, chopped
1 (2-ounce) jar chopped pimiento,
   rinsed and drained
¾ to 1 cup sugar (depending on
   taste)
1 cup cider vinegar
2 tablespoons sugar
1 teaspoon salt
1 teaspoon celery seed
1 teaspoon dry mustard
¾ cup vegetable oil

Place cabbage in a 13x9-inch glass baking dish. Layer the green pepper, onion, and pimiento over the cabbage. Sprinkle with ¾ to 1 cup sugar. Do not stir. Make dressing by placing vinegar, 2 tablespoons sugar, salt, celery seed, and dry mustard in a saucepan and bringing to a boil. Add the vegetable oil and bring to a boil again. Remove from the heat and cool to lukewarm. Pour over the cabbage mixture. Do not stir. Cover and refrigerate at least 4 hours. Stir before serving and serve with a slotted spoon. Makes 8-10 servings.

NOTE: This cole slaw lasts up to one week tightly covered in the refrigerator.

Garden Pasta Salad

1 pound thin spaghetti
3 carrots, chopped and blanched (see note)
2 cups chopped broccoli flowerets
2 scallions including green tops, chopped
2 tomatoes, chopped
1 (4½-ounce) can chopped ripe olives
½ cup (4 ounces) bottled Italian salad dressing
1 (.07-ounce) package dry Italian salad dressing mix
Parmesan cheese according to taste

Cook spaghetti according to package directions. While it is cooking, prepare the vegetables. When spaghetti is done, drain and rinse under cold water. Immediately add the bottled Italian dressing and the dry Italian salad dressing mix. Toss in vegetables and mix all together. Serves 8-10 as main dish or 10-12 as a side dish.

NOTE: To blanch carrots, fill a small saucepan with water and bring to a boil. Drop in chopped carrots, let water return to a boil, and boil for 15 seconds. Drain carrots and rinse under cold water.

– Debby Mitchell

Creamy Ranch Potato Salad

1 cup ranch or lite ranch salad dressing
½ cup sliced green onions
2 tablespoons snipped fresh dillweed
1 teaspoon Dijon-style mustard
2 hard-cooked eggs, finely chopped
½ teaspoon salt
¼ teaspoon pepper
3 pounds Red Bliss or new potatoes, cooked and cut into large chunks and kept warm

In a large salad bowl thoroughly combine all ingredients except the potatoes. Toss in the warm potatoes; cover and chill. Makes about 10 side-dish servings.

– Barb Garside

Exotic Wild Rice Salad
Make ahead for flavor to meld

2⅓ cups raw wild or brown rice or
    a combination
1 cups currants or dried red
    cherries
5 celery stalks, finely diced
4 carrots, peeled and finely diced
1 large red onion, diced
1 large shallot, minced
1 small red bell pepper, diced
1 small yellow bell pepper, diced
⅔ cup chopped parsley
1 cup extra-virgin olive oil
¼ cup balsamic vinegar
½ teaspoon black pepper

Cook rice according to package directions. If using currants, plump in warm water for 20-30 minutes; drain. In a large bowl combine the rice, currants or cherries, celery, carrots, onion, shallot, red and yellow pepper, and parsley. In a small bowl combine the olive oil, vinegar and black pepper and whisk to blend. Pour dressing over the salad and coat well. Serve at room temperature. If serving later, refrigerate, but let stand 1 hour before serving in order for salad to return to room temperature. Serves 10-12.

NOTE: Exotic it is but enjoyed by nearly everyone. It's a terrific buffet salad and great for parties because it can be made ahead.

Tabouleh
(Bulgur Wheat and Parsley Salad)
Vegetarians will love this

⅓ cup bulgur wheat
Hot water to cover wheat
2 medium-sized tomatoes, peeled
    and diced
4 tablespoons minced onions
2 loosely packed cups finely
    chopped parsley
3 tablespoons fresh lemon juice
1 teaspoon salt
2 tablespoons olive oil
Crisp inner leaves from a head of
    romaine lettuce

Soak bulgur wheat in hot water to cover for 20 minutes. Drain the liquid from the wheat. Add the tomatoes, onion, parsley, lemon juice, salt, and oil to the bulgur wheat and mix well. Taste and adjust seasonings if needed. To serve, place in the center of lettuce leaves. Chill for 1 hour. Serves 4.

– Joanne Ehrlich

Chicken Salad

A taste of the Far East

4 fryers, cooked and cut into
 bite-size pieces
2 (8-ounce) cans water chestnuts,
 drained
2 pounds seedless grapes, halved
2 cups sliced celery
Toasted almonds to taste
Pineapple chunks to taste

Dressing

3 cups mayonnaise
1 tablespoon curry powder
2 tablespoons soy sauce
2 tablespoons lemon juice

Mix chicken, water chestnuts, grapes, celery, almonds, and pineapple together. Mix dressing ingredients together and add to chicken salad mixture. Chill. Serves 18.

– Penny Edson

Far East Chicken Salad

Pretty served in cantaloupe half

1 (3 to 4 pound) chicken or 6
 chicken breast halves
Onion and celery leaves for
 poaching
1 cup white rice
3 to 4 tablespoons chopped onion
1 teaspoon curry powder (may add
 more to taste)
1 teaspoon salt
1 teaspoon vinegar
2 tablespoons corn oil
1 cup chopped celery
1 cup frozen green peas
 (unthawed)
1 cup mayonnaise
1 (6-ounce) bag toasted almonds
1 cup green grapes, halved
1 (16¼-ounce) can pineapple
 tidbits

Place chicken in a cooking pot; add water to cover along with onion and celery leaves. Bring water to a boil and simmer for ½ hour or until done. Remove chicken from heat and let cool in broth. Remove chicken from broth, bone and cut into bite-size pieces; reserve. Meanwhile cook the rice. When rice is done, add chopped onion, curry powder, salt, vinegar, and corn oil and mix well; refrigerate. When ready to serve, add celery, peas, mayonnaise, almonds, grapes, pineapple, and chicken to the rice mixture. Makes 12 servings.

NOTE: Everything except the grapes and pineapple can be mixed together ahead - add them just before serving.

– Suzy Harlan

Chicken Cole Slaw

2 cups shredded green cabbage
2 cups diced cooked chicken
1 cup unpeeled, cubed red apple
1 cup seedless red grapes, halved
½ cup sliced celery
½ cup chopped walnuts
½ cup sour cream
3 tablespoons mayonnaise
3 tablespoons honey
1 tablespoon lemon juice
⅛ teaspoon salt
Dash of pepper
Leaf lettuce (optional)

Combine first 6 ingredients in a large bowl; set aside. Combine all of the rest of the ingredients except the lettuce and blend until smooth. Pour over the chicken mixture and toss gently. Cover and chill 1-2 hours. To serve, spoon cole slaw into a lettuce-lined bowl if desired. Serves 6.

– Susan Ferrell

Marinated Chicken Pasta Salad

¼ cup wine vinegar
2 teaspoons Dijon mustard
2 teaspoons chopped garlic
Salt and pepper to taste
½ cup French olive oil
½ pound vermicelli, broken in half, cooked in salted water for 4 minutes and drained
1 (3-pound) chicken or 4 whole chicken breasts, cooked and chopped
1 cup mayonnaise
Minced parsley
Optional: canned marinated artichokes, black olives, etc. for garnish

Mix vinegar, mustard, garlic, salt and pepper together. Whisk in olive oil. Pour dressing over cooked vermicelli in large bowl. Combine chicken and mayonnaise and add to vermicelli mixture. Refrigerate overnight. To serve, place on large platter and garnish with chopped parsley. May surround with marinated vegetables.

– Becky Dunn

Terry's Tuna Sunshine Salad
Delightful luncheon dish

8 ounces seashell pasta, cooked
    and drained
1 cup mayonnaise
1 (6½-ounce) can tuna, drained
    and flaked
1 (11-ounce) can mandarin
    oranges, drained
⅓ cup chopped sweet gherkins
⅓ cup seedless raisins
2 tablespoons lemon juice
1 teaspoon salt

Gently toss all of the ingredients together. Cover and chill. Makes about 6 cups.

NOTE: Oranges make this tuna salad more refreshing than most.

French Salad Dressing
An original recipe from a French Canadian

½ cup sugar
2 tablespoons grated onions
2 teaspoons salt
⅛ teaspoon dry mustard
1 teaspoon Worcestershire sauce
4 tablespoons water
4 tablespoons catsup
4 tablespoons wine vinegar
1 cup pure vegetable oil

Mix all ingredients except the oil in a blender and blend. When well blended, add the oil and mix again. Serve over your favorite green or spinach salad. Makes about 2 cups.

– Gigi Roberts

Raspberry Vinaigrette
A spectacular smash

Juice of ½ a lemon
¼ cup raspberry or champagne
    vinegar
½ cup fresh raspberries
½ cup vegetable oil

Combine lemon juice and vinegar in a blender. Add berries; puree until smooth. With machine running, add oil in a steady stream. Makes about 1 cup.

NOTE: This dressing makes an elegant finish for an endive-watercress salad. Or drizzle over fruit or chicken salad.

– Hazel Bunt-Sandoval

SOUPS AND STEWS

Cream of Broccoli Soup

Yummy!

2 (10-ounce) packages frozen
  chopped broccoli
2 (10¾-ounce) cans cream of
  mushroom soup, undiluted
2⅔ cups milk
3 tablespoons butter or margarine
¼ to ½ teaspoon dried tarragon
Dash pepper

Cook broccoli according to package directions; drain well. Add remaining ingredients and cook over low heat until thoroughly heated. Makes about 8 cups.

– Linda Stevenson

Fresh Mushroom Soup

⅓ cup plus 2 teaspoons diced
  onion
1 tablespoon plus 1 teaspoon
  enriched flour
2 cups sliced mushrooms
2 cups water
1 packet instant chicken broth and
  seasoning mix
⅛ teaspoon ground thyme
Dash each salt and pepper
2 teaspoons chopped fresh parsley

Spray saucepan with nonstick cooking spray. Add onion; cook stirring occasionally, about 5 minutes or until softened. Stir in flour and cook until mixture is lightly browned. Add mushrooms; cook 5 minutes. Stir in water, broth mix, and thyme. Bring mixture to a boil; reduce heat and simmer 10 minutes or until slightly thickened. Season with salt and pepper. Just before serving, sprinkle with parsley. Serves 2.

– Connie Cavett

Garden Soup

2 (14½-ounce) cans chicken broth, undiluted
2 (11½-ounce) cans tomato juice
2 cups chopped, cooked chicken
1 (12-ounce) can whole kernel corn, drained (or frozen equivalent, thawed)
1 (10-ounce) package frozen lima beans, thawed
2 to 4 small potatoes, peeled and chopped
1 medium onion, chopped
½ cup finely chopped celery
½ cup finely chopped carrots
1½ tablespoons Worcestershire sauce
1 bay leaf
¾ teaspoon garlic salt
½ teaspoon pepper

Combine all ingredients in a large Dutch oven. Bring to a boil. Cover, reduce heat, and simmer 1 hour, stirring occasionally. Yield: 11 cups.

– Laurie Farquharson

Chili

Serve with corn bread

1 pound ground round
½ cup chopped green pepper
½ cup chopped onion
1 (10¾-ounce) can tomato soup
1 (16-ounce) can tomatoes
1 clove garlic, minced
1 tablespoon chili powder (or to taste)
⅛ teaspoon cayenne pepper
½ teaspoon paprika
1 bay leaf
1 (16-ounce) can red kidney beans, undrained
Salt to taste

Brown the ground round, green pepper and onion until brown; drain. Add tomato soup, tomatoes, garlic, chili powder, cayenne pepper, paprika and bay leaf. Simmer uncovered for 1 hour, stirring occasionally. (If needed add water to thin out.) Add beans and salt and heat through. Serves 6.

– Beth Infantino

Midwestern Steak Soup

A ski lodge specialty

1 pound lean ground beef or
   ground sirloin
1 tablespoon dry vermouth
1 stick (4 ounces) margarine
1 cup flour
8 cups (2 quarts) water
1 cup diced onions
1 cup diced carrots
1 cup diced celery
2 cups fresh or frozen vegetables
   of choice
1 (16-ounce) can Italian-style plum
   tomatoes
2 tablespoons beef base
1 teaspoon salt
1 teaspoon black pepper

Sauté ground beef with dry vermouth until brown. Drain any grease. Reserve meat. Melt margarine in a large soup kettle; gradually add flour and stir until well blended. Add the rest of the ingredients and bring to a boil. Add reserved meat. Lower heat and simmer for 45 minutes or until vegetables are cooked to taste. Makes 4-6 servings.

NOTE: Any vegetable may be used for the extra 2 cups. Broccoli and cabbage are particularly successful. Serve this soup as a main course with bread.

Oven Stew

Outstanding!

2 pounds beef chuck cut into
   2-inch cubes
1 onion, quartered
4 carrots, pared and cut in half
4 celery stalks, quartered
½ green pepper, chopped into
   large pieces
¼ cup quick cooking minute
   tapioca
¼ cup bread crumbs
2 cups (½ pound fresh) whole
   mushrooms
1 teaspoon salt
1 teaspoon pepper
1 (1-pound, 12-ounce) can
   tomatoes
¾ cup red wine

Combine all ingredients in Dutch oven with a tight cover. Cook at 300°F for 4 hours. Don't uncover until done. Makes 8 servings.

NOTE: Do try this recipe. It gives one time to play a match, return, and shower before serving.

– Becky Dunn

Pressure Cooker Beef Stew

Back in style

1 pound stew beef, trimmed
1 medium onion, sliced
Olive oil for sautéing beef and
  onion
4 carrots, cut into bite-size pieces
1 cup string beans, cut into pieces
4 small potatoes, cubed
3 to 4 tomatoes, peeled and
  chopped
1 cup water
1 beef bouillon cube
Salt and pepper to taste

Brown the meat and onions in olive oil in pressure cooker, stirring over brisk heat. Add the other ingredients. Close cooker and bring to "boil" (where the top rocks); then reduce heat to gentle rocking. Cook for 10 more minutes. Remove from the heat and reduce pressure before opening. If the stew is too thin, simmer uncovered a while longer. Makes 4 main dish servings.

NOTE: Pressure cookers are back in style because of their time-saving properties. Lots of new, safer models are on the market now. This recipe is easy to double - but make each batch one at a time in the pressure cooker.

– Barbara Ferrero

Roochio's Lentil Soup

2 cups dried lentils
8 cups water
2 tablespoons salt
1 teaspoon marjoram
½ cup olive oil
8 onions, chopped
8 carrots, diced
1 cup chopped fresh parsley or
  ¾ cup dried parsley
2 (10-ounce) cans RoTel tomatoes
  and green chilies
2 tablespoons sherry
½ (6-ounce) can tomato paste
½ cup grated Gruyere or jack
  cheese

Soak lentils overnight. Rinse twice. Cover with water. Add spices, bring to a boil and reduce heat. Simmer 1 hour. Saute onions and carrots slowly in oil. Add to lentils along with parsley, tomatoes, sherry, tomato paste, and cheese. Serve with French bread and a green salad. Makes 4 main dish servings.

NOTE: A delicious lentil soup without a bit of ham or bacon

Black Bean Soup
Vegetarian main dish

1 pound black beans
2 quarts water
1 tablespoon salt
2 tablespoons olive oil
1 large onion, chopped
1 large green pepper, chopped
2 cloves garlic, minced
1 teaspoon salt
1 teaspoon ground cumin
1 teaspoon oregano leaves
¼ teaspoon dry mustard
1 tablespoon lemon juice

Rinse and pick through beans. Soak beans in the water overnight. When ready to cook, use the same water the beans were soaked in and add 1 tablespoon salt; bring to a boil, cover and cook until the beans are almost tender - about 1 hour. When the beans are almost done, heat olive oil in skillet and sauté onion for 5 minutes; add green pepper and continue sautéing until the onions are tender. While onions and green pepper are cooking, crush together the garlic, salt, cumin, oregano and dry mustard. Stir this mixture, along with lemon juice and about ½ cup of the hot bean liquid, into the onions and green pepper. Cover and simmer for 10 minutes. Add to the beans and continue cooking for 1 more hour.

To thicken the soup, remove 2 cups of the beans and liquid and puree in a blender or food processor, returning puree to soup.

Serve in bowl with mounds of hot dry rice in the center. For garnish provide chopped raw onion. Serves 8.

– Edie Fagan

MEAT

Beef Brisket
Guests will ask for the recipe

4 to 5 pounds beef brisket
1 medium onion, sliced and
   separated into rings
1 envelope onion soup mix
1 cup water
1 cup barbecue sauce
6 medium-size potatoes, peeled
   and cut in half
1 (12-ounce) can beer

Brown brisket on all sides in small amount of cooking oil. Drain off grease. Add cut onion to the meat. Mix package of onion soup and all liquids except beer. Pour on top of meat and cook at medium to low heat for 1 hour and 30 minutes to 2 hours. Add potatoes and beer and cook 30 minutes to 45 minutes until potatoes are cooked. Serve with white rice. Serves 10-12.

NOTE: This dish can be made the day ahead and warmed up on the stove just before serving.

– Alina Avello

Barbecued Beef Brisket
It doesn't get any easier

1 (4-pound) beef brisket, fat
   trimmed
1 (4-ounce) bottle liquid smoke
1 (18-ounce) bottle barbecue sauce

Spray a 13x9-inch pan with no stick cooking spray. Put meat in pan and cover with the liquid smoke. Cover the pan with aluminum foil and bake at 250°F for 5 hours. Pour off all but ½ cup of the liquid. Slice the meat in 1-inch slices *across* the grain. Pour the barbecue sauce over the meat and refrigerate overnight. To serve, place the covered pan in a 250°F oven and cook for 1 hour. Serves 10-12.

– Karen Rock

15-Minute Stroganoff
Great family dish

1 pound round steak trimmed
  of fat
3 tablespoons butter
⅔ cup water
1 (3-ounce) can mushrooms,
  undrained
1 package onion soup mix
1 (8-ounce) carton (1 cup) sour
  cream
2 tablespoons flour
Hot cooked rice or noodles

Cut meat into ¼-inch strips across the grain. Brown the strips quickly in butter. Add water and mushrooms. Stir in soup mix and heat to just boiling. Blend in sour cream and flour and stir until mixture thickens. Serve over rice or noodles. Serves 4.

– Jenny McKenna

Mezzeti (Ground Beef Casserole)
A dish with a past

4 ounces uncooked narrow egg
  noodles
1 pound ground beef
1 medium green pepper, chopped
1 medium onion, chopped
1 (12¾-ounce) can tomato soup
1 (4-ounce) can sliced mushrooms
½ cup Cheddar cheese

Cook noodles according to package directions. Cook ground beef, green pepper, and onions until meat is cooked and vegetables are tender. Add soup and mushrooms and fold in noodles. Place in a 9-inch square baking dish and top with cheese. Bake at 350°F for 30-35 minutes. Serves 4.

NOTE: This is a casserole with a mysterious past. We've traced it from Virginia to Denver with many different spellings and variations such as Johnny Mozetti, Mosetti, Marazotti, etc. If you can shed any light on this fellow, do let us know.

– Betty Guthrie

Parmesan Meat Bundles

2 pounds ground beef
½ cup soft bread crumbs
¼ cup chopped onion
1 teaspoon salt
¼ teaspoon pepper
1 cup cooked and drained thin
   noodles
1 cup shredded mozzarella cheese
¼ cup grated Parmesan cheese
1 tablespoon chopped parsley
1 (16-ounce) jar spaghetti sauce
2 tablespoons grated Parmesan
   cheese

Combine meat, crumbs, onion and seasonings. Mix lightly. Divide meat mixture into 6 portions. On wax paper, shape each portion into a 6-inch patty. In a bowl, combine noodles, mozzarella cheese, ¼ cup Parmesan cheese, and parsley; toss lightly. Place approximately ⅓ cup of the noodle mixture in the center of each patty. Bake at 375°F for 30 minutes. Drain. Pour spaghetti sauce over the meat. Sprinkle tops with Parmesan cheese. Cook at 350°F for 25 minutes. Makes 6 servings.

NOTE: These may be cooked and frozen. To serve, remove from freezer and thaw. Cover dish and cook in microwave until heated through.

– Esther Treese

Pork Chops 'n Sauce
Real easy and real good

1 envelope onion soup mix
1 envelope mushroom gravy mix
1 cup water
No stick cooking spray
8 thin pork chops, trimmed of fat

Mix onion soup mix, mushroom gravy mix, and water in a small saucepan and heat. Meanwhile, spray frying pan with cooking spray and quickly brown pork chops over high heat. Place 4 browned pork chops in a 10x10-inch square baking dish. Pour half of the onion soup/ gravy mixture over the pork chops. Place the remaining 4 browned pork chops over the others and cover with the rest of the onion soup/ gravy mixture. Bake at 350°F for about 1 hour. Serve with rice. Serves 4.

– Betty Guthrie

Enchilada Casserole
No-hassle Tex-Mex

1 pound ground round or sirloin
1 small onion, chopped
1 (8-ounce) can tomato sauce
½ teaspoon garlic powder
1 teaspoon chili powder
Salt to taste
1 (4-ounce) can chopped ripe
  olives
1 (4-ounce) can chopped green
  chilies
5 (8-inch) flour tortillas
2 teaspoons liquid margarine
1 cup (4 ounces) grated Cheddar
  cheese
⅔ cup water

Brown the meat and onion in a skillet; drain any grease. Add the tomato sauce, garlic powder, chili powder, salt, olives, and green chilies and mix well. Remove from the heat. Cut or tear the tortillas into quarters. Spray a 9x9-inch baking dish with non-stick vegetable spray. Line the bottom of the dish with ½ of the tortillas and cover with ½ of the meat sauce. Place the remaining tortillas over the meat sauce and squeeze the liquid margarine over them. Cover with the remaining meat sauce and sprinkle the cheese over the top. Pour the water around the edges of the pan. Bake at 350°F for 40 minutes. Serves 4-6.

Picadillo
Spanish culinary delight

2 pounds ground round or sirloin
1 tablespoon olive oil
2 medium onions, chopped
1 large green pepper, chopped
2 (16-ounce) cans tomatoes,
  crushed
2 teaspoons salt
1 teaspoon garlic powder
½ teaspoon pepper
1 tablespoon brown sugar
¼ cup vinegar
¼ cup stuffed green olives,
  chopped
½ cup raisins
1 tablespoon capers
½ cup red wine or tomato juice

In a large skillet brown the meat in hot olive oil until the red in meat just disappears. Add the chopped onion and green pepper and cook for another 5 minutes. Add the remaining ingredients and cook over low heat for 45 minutes to 1 hour or until most of the liquid has been absorbed. Serve over hot white rice. Makes 10 servings.

NOTE: Even though there are lots of ingredients this is a very easy dish to prepare. Children love it.

Bleu Cheese Pork Chop Noodle Casserole

3 cups noodles, uncooked
6 (½-inch) pork chops
Salt and pepper to taste
Bleu Cheese Sauce
3 tablespoons butter
3 tablespoons flour
¾ teaspoon salt
Dash pepper
1 cup milk
¾ cup (3 ounces) crumbled bleu
  cheese
3 tablespoons chopped green
  pepper
3 tablespoons chopped pimiento

Cook noodles in boiling water; rinse; drain. Set aside. Brown 6 (½-inch) pork chops on both sides. Season with salt and pepper to taste. Make bleu cheese sauce by melting butter and blending in flour and salt and pepper. Stir in milk and cook, stirring, until thick. Add bleu cheese and stir until cheese melts. Combine noodles, sauce, green peppers and pimientos. Place in 13x9-inch baking dish. Arrange pork chops on top. Bake at 350°F about 30 minutes or until done. Makes 6 servings.

– Bonnie Harwell

Chinese Barbecued Spareribs

2 racks meaty pork spareribs
(about 4 pounds) split in half
lengthwise

Marinade

1 cup catsup
2 tablespoons brown sugar
⅓ to ½ cup Hoisin sauce
2 tablespoons soy sauce
2 tablespoons dry sherry
1 clove garlic, minced

Select meaty pork spareribs that are lean and free of excess fat. For serving as a main dish, you will need about 1 pound of ribs per person. Ask the butcher to split the racks of ribs in half lengthwise or, if desired do this at home with a meat cleaver.

Place ribs in a large baking dish. Set ribs aside and make marinade: in a small bowl, mix catsup, brown sugar, Hoisin sauce (to taste), soy sauce, sherry and garlic. Stir to combine thoroughly. Spoon over spareribs and turn ribs to coat evenly. Cover tightly and chill overnight. If possible, turn the ribs and brush them with marinade several times.

Preheat oven 375°F. Remove ribs from refrigerator. Uncover dish and place on center rack in oven. Roast for 1½ hours, turning often and basting frequently. When done, remove pan from oven and cut ribs into serving size pieces. (This can be done ahead; cover and chill ribs until just before serving. Reheat in preheated oven). Makes 4 main dish servings or serves 8 or more as hors d'oeuvres.

– Cindi Steffens

Pork Medallions with Vegetables

Exquisite

1 tablespoon margarine
2 medium green peppers, sliced
2 medium onions, sliced
4 tomatoes, peeled and chopped
   coarsely
1 (6-inch long) pork tenderloin
   (about 3 pounds)
4 tablespoons margarine
½ cup sherry or other dry white
   wine
½ cup heavy whipping cream
Salt and pepper to taste
2 to 3 cups hot cooked rice

Melt 1 tablespoon margarine in a frying pan. Add green peppers, onions, and tomatoes and simmer over medium low heat. When vegetables have simmered for 10 minutes turn heat to low and cover pan. Continue to simmer the vegetables while beginning to cook the pork medallions in a separate frying pan. Prepare the pork medallions by melting 4 tablespoons margarine over medium high heat (325°F if using an electric skillet). Add medallions and sauté for 5 minutes on each side; season each side of the medallions with salt and pepper to taste. When medallions are done, remove from the pan to a serving platter. Pour the sherry into the pan from which the medallions were removed. Boil sherry down rapidly to reduce by about half. Immediately add the cream and boil a minute or two to thicken slightly. Pour the sauce over the medallions. Serve by placing vegetables on hot cooked rice and topping with pork medallions and cream sauce. Serves 4-6 depending on the rest of your menu.

NOTE: To peel tomatoes, bring 3 quarts of water to a boil. Drop tomatoes in boiling water for 10 seconds. Remove and peel. Easy!

– Astrid Alexander

Greek Lamb Shanks
Healthy fare

4 lamb shanks
1 large onion, sliced thin
1½ tablespoons minced garlic
1 cup chopped green peppers
1½ cups diced carrots
⅛ cup dried dill
2 bay leaves
2 teaspoons dried oregano
1 teaspoon dried thyme
Grated rind of 1 lemon
2 cups tomato sauce
1 cup dry white wine
Pepper to taste

Preheat oven to 375°F. Place lamb in an ovenproof dish in one layer. Distribute next 4 ingredients over the lamb. Mix together dill, bay leaves, oregano, thyme, lemon rind, tomato sauce, and wine. Pour over lamb. Cover and bake 70 minutes. Lower heat to 350°F and bake for 30 minutes. Increase heat to 400°F; uncover and turn shanks. Return to oven and bake 10 minutes. Remove shanks. Skim off fat on surface of sauce. Serve lamb with sauce over rice. Serves 4.

NOTE: To remove fat, prepare one day ahead so fat will solidify in the refrigerator. Remove the fat. Reheat the lamb shanks.

Veal Chops with Mustard Sauce
Treat for two

2 veal chops, cut 1½ inches thick
4 tablespoons margarine, melted
1½ tablespoons Dijon mustard
¼ teaspoon pepper
1 tablespoon drained capers

Brush the veal chops with a sauce made by combining the melted margarine, mustard, and pepper. Cook chops on a grill or under a preheated oven broiler for 6 minutes. Turn over and brush more sauce on the chops. Top with the capers. Cook 6 more minutes. Makes 2 servings.

NOTE: This sauce is also good served on vegetables. The recipe can be doubled easily.

Baked Lamb Chops en Casserole

A pre-assembled party dish

8 lamb chops (about 2½ pounds)
¼ cup flour
2 tablespoons margarine
2 tablespoons olive oil
½ cup dry white wine
1 cup chicken or beef bouillon
½ teaspoon salt
⅛ teaspoon pepper
½ teaspoon garlic powder
2 tablespoons chopped parsley
¼ teaspoon dried crushed rosemary
4 medium potatoes, peeled and sliced
½ pound fresh mushrooms, sliced
2 medium onions, sliced thinly

Dust chops with flour. Heat margarine and oil in frying pan over medium heat. Brown chops 5 minutes on each side. Remove chops when browned and set aside. In same pan, add wine, bouillon, salt, pepper, garlic powder, parsley, and rosemary. Bring to a boil, stirring to loosen browned bits; set aside. Place potatoes on the bottom of a 13x9-inch casserole. Arrange mushrooms and onions over the potatoes and top with chops. Pour wine mixture over all. Cover and bake at 350°F for 1¼ hours. Makes 6-8 servings.

NOTE: If making ahead, add 15-20 minutes to the baking time. Pork or veal chops can be substituted for the lamb chops.

POULTRY

Kincaid's Chicken Diable

4 tablespoons butter
½ cup honey
¼ cup prepared yellow mustard
1 teaspoon salt
1 teaspoon curry
6 chicken breasts, split and boned

Melt butter. Stir in honey, mustard, salt, and curry and blend until a smooth sauce is formed. Butter a large 3-quart baking dish. Dredge the chicken breasts in the sauce. Arrange chicken in dish. Spoon the remaining sauce over the chicken. Bake at 350°F for 35 minutes. Turn oven up to 500°F and cook for another 8-10 minutes. Serves 12 for lunch - 8 for dinner.

– Sue Kincaid

Chicken Sublime

2 pounds boneless, skinless
   chicken breasts
1 egg, beaten
½ cup bread crumbs
2 tablespoons vegetable oil
½ cup chicken broth
¼ cup white wine
1½ tablespoons lemon juice
2 tablespoons grated Parmesan
   cheese
Salt and pepper to taste
4 to 6 medium-sized fresh
   mushrooms (optional)

Dip chicken breasts in egg and then in bread crumbs. Brown in the oil and place in a 1½-2-quart baking dish. Mix together the broth, wine, and lemon juice and pour into the baking dish. Sprinkle the chicken breasts with the Parmesan cheese, salt and pepper. Add the mushrooms to the baking dish if you wish. Cover and cook 25 minutes at 350°F. Uncover and cook for another 10 minutes. Serves 3.

– Inez St. Pierre

Chicken Piccata
Jet-set favorite

4 chicken breast halves (about
  6-ounces each), skinned and
  boned
¼ cup all purpose flour
¼ cup margarine
¼ cup dry white wine
2 tablespoons lemon juice
½ teaspoon salt
Pepper to taste
Lemon slices and parsley sprigs
  as garnish

Pound chicken to ½-inch thickness. Coat chicken with flour. Melt the margarine in a large skillet over medium heat. Add chicken and cook for 3 minutes per side or until lightly browned. Add wine, lemon juice, salt, and pepper; bring to a boil. Reduce the heat and simmer, uncovered for 3 minutes or until the sauce is slightly thickened. Remove the chicken to a serving dish and pour the sauce over the top. Garnish with lemon slices and parsley if you wish. Serves 2-4.

Chicken Supreme
Shrimp can be substituted

4 whole (8 half) chicken breasts,
  skinned and boned
1 envelope onion soup mix
1 (10-ounce) jar apricot preserves
1 (8-ounce) bottle Russian salad
  dressing
½ cup sherry cooking wine
½ teaspoon powdered ginger

Wash chicken breasts and pat dry. Place in an 8½x12-inch glass baking dish. Mix remaining ingredients together and pour over the chicken. Bake at 375°F for 30-35 minutes. (Do not overcook or chicken will be tough.) Good served with white or wild rice. Serves 4-6.

NOTE: To divide this recipe, use 4 chicken breasts halves and ½ (2¼ cups) of the sauce. Save the sauce for another use. You can also substitute shrimp for the chicken. Marinate the shrimp in the sauce for several hours and then bake in a 400°F oven for about 5 minutes per side or just until the shrimp are pink and tender.

– Betty Guthrie

Chicken Shrimp Supreme

For family or *guests*

¼ cup butter
½ pound sliced mushrooms
2 tablespoons chopped green onions
2 (10¾-ounce) cans cream of chicken soup
½ cup vermouth
½ cup light cream or Half & Half
1 cup Cheddar cheese
2 cups cooked chicken
2 cups cooked shrimp
3 tablespoons parsley

In saucepan melt butter. Add mushrooms and green onions and sauté five minutes. Add soup; gradually stir in vermouth and cream. Add cheese and heat over low heat, stirring occasionally, until cheese is melted. Add chicken and shrimp; heat to serving temperature - do not boil. Just before serving, stir in parsley. Serve over rice. Serves 6-8.

– Susan Schwarzrock

Hot Chicken Salad

½ cup sliced almonds
1 tablespoon margarine
2 cups diced, cooked chicken
1 cup diced celery
½ teaspoon salt
2 teaspoons grated onion
½ cup mayonnaise
½ cup undiluted cream of mushroom soup
½ cup grated Cheddar cheese
½ cup crushed potato chips

Sauté almonds in margarine; drain. Combine all other ingredients except potato chips. Spoon into a lightly greased 1-quart casserole. Sprinkle with potato chips. Bake at 425°F for 20 minutes. Serves 6.

– Susan Scott

Chicken Pot Pie

Makes an imposing presentation

1 (4-pound) chicken
4 hard boiled eggs
1½ cups chopped celery

White Sauce

¼ cup margarine
¼ cup flour
½ teaspoon Beau Monde
   seasoning
2 cups milk

Crust

2 cups flour
3 teaspoons baking powder
½ teaspoon salt
1 cup grated Cheddar cheese
½ cup oil
⅔ cup milk

Cook chicken in boiling water to cover until done, about ½ hour. Tear meat off the bone and cut into bite-size pieces. Place chicken, celery, and chopped eggs in a 9x13-inch glass dish. To make a white sauce melt margarine, stir in flour and seasonings. Stir in the 2 cups milk and stir while cooking over medium heat until thick. Pour white sauce over the chicken. Mix all ingredients for the crust. Roll or pat into "pan-cakes" about ½-inch thick and cover the top of the other ingredients. Bake at 425°F for 25-30 minutes. Serves 6-8.

NOTE: For a pretty presentation, roll the crust ¼-inch thick; cut into 3x3x3-inch triangles and roll up as croissants. Place on the top of the filling so that "croissants" just touch.

– Connie Cavett

Chicken Pie

Deliciously peppery

1 (3-pound) fryer
2 tablespoons chopped onion
2 stalks celery with leaves
2 chicken bouillon cubes
1 (10¾-ounce) can cream of celery
  soup
½ cup chicken stock
1 cup flour
2 teaspoons baking powder
¾ teaspoon salt
1 teaspoon pepper
1 stick margarine, melted
1 cup milk

Cook chicken in water to cover along with onion, celery and bouillon cubes. Bring water to a boil and simmer chicken for ½ hour or until done. Remove chicken and reserve stock. Bone chicken and place in 9x11-inch casserole dish. Mix soup and chicken stock and pour over chicken. Make batter by combining the rest of the ingredients. Pour batter over chicken. Bake at 350°F for 30-35 minutes or until lightly browned. Serves 4.

– Becky Dunn

Quick Chicken à la King

A family favorite

½ cup chopped onion
2 tablespoons butter or margarine
1 (8-ounce) package cream
  cheese, softened
1 (10¾-ounce) can cream of
  mushroom soup
Dash pepper
2 (5-ounce) cans boned cooked
  chicken, diced
1 (3-ounce) can broiled sliced
  mushrooms with liquid
¼ cup chopped green pepper
2 tablespoons chopped pimiento
Hot biscuits

Cook onion in butter until tender but not brown. Blend in softened cream cheese, cream of mushroom soup, and pepper. Stir in boned chicken and slice mushrooms with liquid. Heat to boiling. Add green pepper and pimiento. Serve over hot biscuits. Serves 6.

– Gail Loeffler

Chicken Puffs
A lovely luncheon dish

1 (3-ounce) package cream
  cheese, softened
2 tablespoons margarine, melted
2 tablespoons milk
2 cups cubed cooked chicken
¼ teaspoon salt
⅛ teaspoon pepper
1 tablespoon chopped chives
1 (3-ounce) can sliced
  mushrooms, drained
1 (8-ounce) can crescent dinner
  rolls
2 to 3 tablespoons mayonnaise
¾ cup crushed seasoned croutons

Blend cream cheese, margarine, and milk. Add next 5 ingredients and reserve. Separate crescent roll dough into 4 rectangles. Evenly divide chicken mixture among the rectangles. Pull the 4 corners of each rectangle to top center of the chicken mixture, twist slightly and seal edges. Brush tops of each puff with the mayonnaise and sprinkle with crushed croutons. Bake at 350°F for 25 minutes. Makes 4 servings.

– Ellen Koenig

Chinese Chicken

2 cups diced cooked chicken
1 cup diced celery
1 cup raw rice, cooked
¾ cup mayonnaise
1 cup sliced fresh mushrooms
1 teaspoon lemon juice
1 teaspoon chopped onion
1 teaspoon salt
1 (10¾-ounce) can cream of
  chicken soup
1 (4-ounce) can water chestnuts,
  slivered and drained
½ cup butter or margarine
½ cup slivered almonds
1 cup corn flakes

Mix all ingredients except butter, almonds and corn flakes together. Put in 2-quart casserole. Melt butter; add almonds and corn flakes. Sprinkle this mixture on top of casserole. Bake at 350°F for 35 minutes. Serves 6.

NOTE: An excellent casserole which is just as good warmed over the next day.

– Susan Scott

Quick & Easy Oriental Chicken

Delicious, easy, and healthy - who could want more?

1 tablespoon oil
1 onion, chopped (optional)
½ to 1 pound skinless, boneless
   chicken fillets, cut into strips
1 (14-ounce) package Bird's Eye
   Vegetables with Delicate Herb
   Sauce
1 cup cooked rice

Sauté chicken strips and onion in oil in skillet until lightly browned. Add vegetables and stir over low heat to blend sauce cubes. Cover and simmer 5 minutes. Serve over rice. Serves 6.

– Marilyn Brady

Chicken Casserole

Hash browns featured

6 to 7 chicken breast halves,
   cooked and cut into bite-size
   pieces
1 (10¾-ounce) can cream of
   mushroom soup
1 (8-ounce) carton sour cream
1 (8-ounce) package (2 cups)
   shredded Cheddar cheese
1 (7-ounce) package (4 patties in
   package) Orelda Toaster Hash
   Browns, thawed just enough to
   break into bite-size pieces
2½ cups corn flakes
1 stick butter or margarine,
   melted

Combine the first 5 ingredients and place in a 13x11-inch greased baking dish. Gently stir the corn flakes into the melted butter or margarine and spread over the chicken mixture. Bake uncovered at 350°F for 35-40 minutes. (If making in advance, bake the casserole without the topping - when ready to reheat, place the topping on the casserole and put in 350°F oven until warmed through.) Serves 6-8.

– Gunda Fletcher

Deceptive Dinner
Too simple to be believed

1 (10¾-ounce) can cream of
  mushroom soup
1 (10¾-ounce) can cream of
  chicken soup
1 envelope onion soup mix
2 soup cans water
1 cup rice
6 to 7 pieces chicken

Mix all soup ingredients with water; stir in rice. Place in a 13x9-inch baking dish. Place chicken pieces on top of the soup and rice mixture. Bake at 350°F for 1 hour. Makes 4-6 servings.

– Maggie Cosmillo

Chicken with Artichokes
For an elegant dinner party

14 chicken breast halves, boned
  and skinned
2 tablespoons salt
2 teaspoons paprika
1 teaspoon pepper
¾ cup butter
1½ pounds fresh mushrooms
8 tablespoons flour
2 (10¾-ounce) cans chicken broth
1 cup cooking sherry
4 (6-ounce) jars marinated
  artichoke hearts, drained

Preheat oven to 375°F. Mix salt, pepper and paprika. Sprinkle mixture on each piece of chicken. Fry chicken in ½ the butter until brown. Place in a shallow casserole. Add the rest of the butter to frying pan and sauté mushrooms for about 5 minutes or until lightly brown. Sprinkle flour over the mushrooms and mix. Add chicken broth and cooking sherry to mushrooms. Pour mixture over the chicken and add drained artichoke hearts to the casserole. Cover and cook in preheated oven for 40 minutes. Serve with your favorite rice. Serves 10-12.

– Gigi Roberts

Chicken and Marinated Artichokes en Casserole

Even kids love this fancy dish

1 (14-ounce) can marinated
  artichoke hearts, drained
  (2 cups) - reserve marinade
3 cups bite-size pieces of skinned
  and boned chicken breast
2 tablespoons butter
¼ cup artichoke marinade
Salt and pepper to taste
1½ cups shredded Cheddar cheese
4 tablespoons freshly grated
  Parmesan cheese

Preheat oven to 350°F. Sauté the chicken in butter for 3 minutes. Add the artichoke marinade and salt and pepper. Continue cooking until the chicken pieces are barely white all over. Place the chicken in a 13x9-inch baking dish along with the artichoke hearts and cover with the cheeses. Bake in preheated 350°F oven for 30 minutes or until the cheese is brown and bubbly. Serves 4-6.

– Sher Kreisler

Chicken Breasts Italiano

An unusual recipe

4 chicken breast halves, skinned
  and boned
3 tablespoons Italian-style bread
  crumbs
2 tablespoons olive oil
1 (19-ounce) can minestrone soup
2 tablespoons wine vinegar
⅛ teaspoon sugar
1 (14-ounce) can artichoke hearts,
  drained and halved
½ cup chopped parsley

Lightly coat the chicken breasts with bread crumbs. Heat the oil in a large skillet and add the chicken; sauté until brown on both sides. Combine the soup, vinegar, and sugar; pour over the chicken. Simmer, covered, for 10 minutes or until the chicken is cooked. Add the artichoke heart halves and parsley to the skillet and heat through. Serves 4.

NOTE: This out of the ordinary chicken can be served over spaghetti.

Chicken and Broccoli Casserole

Embarassing - it's so easy but gets rave reviews

4 whole chicken breasts (8 halves)
3 (20-ounce) bags frozen chopped
  broccoli
2 (10¾-ounce) cans cream of
  chicken soup
1 cup mayonnaise
¾ teaspoon curry powder
1 teaspoon lemon juice
2 cups shredded sharp Cheddar
  cheese
1 cup (or to taste) plain croutons

Cook chicken in water to cover; bring water to a boil and simmer for 18-20 minutes. Drain and cut into bite-size pieces. While chicken is cooking, cook broccoli according to package directions; drain. Make sauce by mixing together the soup, mayonnaise, curry powder, and lemon juice. Place the broccoli on the bottom of a 9x13-inch pan. Cover the broccoli with the chicken pieces and cover all with the sauce. Bake at 350°F for 30 minutes. Sprinkle the croutons over the top of the casserole and bake for another 5 minutes. Serves 8.

–Martha Smith

Chicken Divan

2 (10-ounce) packages frozen
  broccoli spears, cooked and
  drained
2 cups cooked chicken
2 (10¾-ounce) cans cream of
  chicken soup
1 cup mayonnaise
1 teaspoon lemon juice
½ teaspoon curry powder
½ to 1 cup shredded Cheddar
  cheese (according to taste)
½ cup soft bread crumbs
1 tablespoon melted butter

Arrange cooked broccoli spears in greased 13x9-inch baking dish. Place chicken on top of broccoli. Combine the soup, mayonnaise, lemon juice, and curry powder and pour over the chicken. Sprinkle with the cheese. Combine the crumbs and the melted butter and sprinkle over all. Bake at 350°F for 30 minutes or until heated through. Makes 6 servings.

– Cathie Fowler

Chicken and Wild Rice Casserole

Can be halved

6 to 8 chicken breasts
2 (6-ounce) boxes Uncle Ben's
  Wild Rice
1 onion, chopped
2 sticks butter or margarine
3 tablespoons flour
1½ cans cream of chicken soup
  (cream of mushroom soup may
  be substituted)
1 cup milk
½ pound fresh mushrooms, sliced
  or 1 (2.5-ounce) jar sliced
  mushrooms
1 pound sharp Cheddar cheese,
  shredded

Cook chicken breasts in water to cover; bring water to a boil and simmer for 18-20 minutes. Drain and cut into bite-size pieces. Cook rice as directed on package. Sauté onions in butter or margarine; blend in flour, soup, and milk to make sauce. Add mushrooms to sauce. In a 9x13-inch dish, layer rice, chicken, and sauce. Sprinkle cheese over the top. If you wish, casserole can be frozen at this point. When ready to use, remove from freezer and cook as directed below. Bake casserole at 350°F for 25-30 minutes or until bubbly. Serves 12-14.

– Carolyn Nelson

Chicken Cordon Bleu

6 boneless, skinned chicken
  breasts
6 slices ham, deli or packaged
6 slices Swiss cheese, deli or
  packaged
1 (8-ounce) can Franco-American
  Chicken Gravy

Preheat oven to 350°F. Put 1 slice ham and 1 slice cheese into each chicken breast and roll up; secure with a toothpick. Put the rolled-up chicken into a 8½x8½-inch glass baking dish. Pour chicken gravy over the chicken. Bake for 30 minutes. Serves 6.

NOTE: Don't cook longer than 30 minutes or the chicken will over-cook and the cheese will melt into the gravy. Try serving this tasty dish with mashed potatoes.

– Erika Eidam

Chicken Casserole with Sausage and Mushrooms

Stupendous

½ pound pork sausage
½ pound mushrooms, sliced
2 tablespoons butter
½ stick butter
¼ cup all purpose flour
Salt and pepper to taste
2 cups chicken stock
⅔ cup heavy cream
4 whole chicken breasts, cooked, boned, and cut into 2-inch cubes
4 ounces (½ small package) herb seasoned stuffing
½ stick butter, melted

Preheat oven to 350°F. Roll pork sausage into tiny balls. Brown well and drain on paper towels; reserve. Sauté mushrooms in butter and drain; reserve. Make cream sauce by melting ½ stick butter in saucepan. Stir in ¼ cup flour and salt and pepper. Slowly add chicken stock and cream. Heat, stirring constantly, until thickened. Layer chicken, sausage, and mushrooms in a 13x9-inch casserole. Top with cream sauce. Make topping by combining the stuffing and butter; spread evenly over casserole. Bake for 45 minutes. Serves 8.

NOTE: This may look like a complicated recipe. All the steps are quite easy, however, and the results are stupendous.

– Nan Lasbury

No-Fuss Chicken Fajitas

2 tablespoons lemon juice
½ teaspoon salt
¼ teaspoon coarsely ground
  pepper
¼ teaspoon garlic powder
½ teaspoon liquid smoke
3 chicken breast halves, skinned,
  boned and cut into long strips
6 (6-inch) flour tortillas
2 tablespoons vegetable oil
1 green or sweet red pepper, cut
  into strips (may use both red
  and green)
1 medium onion, sliced and
  separated into rings

*Optional accompaniments
(choose some or all):*

Chopped tomatoes, green
onions, lettuce, gaucamole,
sour cream, shredded cheese,
and picante sauce

Combine first 5 ingredients in a small bowl. Add chicken and stir to coat. Cover and chill at least 30 minutes. Drain chicken, reserving marinade. Wrap tortillas in aluminum foil; bake at 350°F for 15 minutes.

Heat oil in a heavy skillet. Add chicken; cook for 2-3 minutes, stirring constantly. Add marinade, peppers, and onion; sauté until vegetables are crisp-tender. Remove from heat. Divide mixture evenly and spoon a portion onto each tortilla. If desired, top with any of the mentioned accompaniments. Makes 6 fajitas (3 servings).

– Gail Loeffler

Turkey à la King

Remedy for after Thanksgiving doldrums

½ cup Fat Free White Sauce Mix
  (see index)
2 cups chicken broth
1 tablespoon margarine
¾ cup canned or fresh sliced
  mushrooms
2 cups cooked turkey chunks
Salt and pepper to taste

Stir together the white sauce mix and broth. Add margarine and heat, stirring, until thick. Add remaining ingredients and heat through. Serve over rice, noodles, toast, or pastry shells. Serves 4.

Turkey Casserole

½ cup chopped onion
½ cup chopped celery
2 tablespoons vegetable oil
2 cups chopped cooked turkey
1 (10¾-ounce) can cream of
 mushroom soup
2 cups chow mein noodles
½ cup chopped almonds or
 cashews

Sauté onions and celery in oil. Combine all other ingredients except ⅔ cup of the noodles and the nuts. Put in 1½-quart casserole. Top with remaining noodles and nuts. Bake at 300°F for 1 hour and 30 minutes. Serves 6.

– Susan Scott

Great Turkey Casserole
Lives up to its name

1 cup white rice
1 small onion, chopped
1 tablespoon vegetable oil
1½ to 2 cups cooked turkey
1 (10¾-ounce) can cream of
 mushroom soup
1 (10-ounce) package frozen peas
2 cups grated Cheddar cheese

Cook rice. Place in a greased 2-quart casserole. Sauté onion in vegetable oil. Mix onion with turkey, soup, and peas. Spread turkey mixture over rice. Sprinkle cheese over all. Bake at 350°F for 20-30 minutes. Serves 6.

– Susan Scott

Easy Turkey Tetrazzini

6 ounces uncooked spaghetti,
 broken into pieces
¼ cup butter or margarine
½ cup all purpose flour
2¾ cups chicken broth
1 cup light cream
1 teaspoon salt
Pepper to taste
1 (6-ounce) can mushrooms,
 drained
¼ cup chopped green pepper
2 cups diced cooked chicken or
 turkey
½ cup shredded Parmesan cheese

Cook spaghetti until just tender; drain. Melt butter or margarine; blend in flour. Stir chicken broth into flour mixture. Add cream; cook and stir until mixture thickens and bubbles. Add salt, pepper, drained mushrooms, green pepper, cooked chicken or turkey and drained spaghetti. Turn into a 12x7-inch baking dish. Sprinkle top with Parmesan cheese. Bake at 350°F about 30 minutes. Makes 5-6 servings.

– Gail Loeffler

Quick Turkey Tetrazzini

4 ounces spaghetti
1 (10-ounce) package frozen peas
2 cups cubed cooked turkey
½ cup grated Parmesan cheese
Paprika to taste

Sauce

1 (10¾-ounce) can cream of
  mushroom soup
1 cup turkey stock
1 cup grated sharp Cheddar
  cheese
½ teaspoon Worcestershire sauce
1 teaspoon salt
⅛ teaspoon pepper

Preheat oven to 350°F. Cook spaghetti until just tender. Drain and rinse. Cook peas and drain. To make sauce, mix all ingredients in a saucepan and heat until the cheese is melted and well blended. Toss spaghetti, peas and turkey in ½ of the sauce and put in a 2-quart baking dish. Pour rest of the sauce over this. Sprinkle with Parmesan cheese and paprika. Bake, uncovered, in preheated oven until bubbly - about 30 minutes. Serves 4.

– Gigi Roberts

Duckling with Sour Red Cherries
For romantic evenings

1 duck
Salt and pepper to taste
Marjoram to taste
2 cups chicken broth
½ cup *Fat Free White Sauce Mix*
  (see index)
2 cups sweet red wine
2 cups canned sour cherries

Season the duck with the salt, pepper and marjoram. Place in a saucepan with the chicken broth and simmer for 1 hour. Remove the skin from the duck and throw away. Strip the meat off of the bones. Make a white sauce by combining the *Fat Free White Sauce Mix* with the red wine. Add the duck and the cherries. Serve over hot cooked rice. Serves 2.

SEAFOOD

Crab Virginia

By way of a Florida restaurant

¼ cup butter
2 tablespoons lemon juice
1 (16-ounce) can crabmeat
Paprika

Preheat oven to 400°F. Mix all ingredients together and place them in a 1-quart casserole or 4 individual shells or ramekins. Sprinkle the top with paprika. Cook for 15 minutes.

This dish can be cooked in the microwave. Substitute 1 ounce of wine for the lemon juice. Mix all ingredients together, place in microwave-safe dish, cover, and cook on high power for 5 minutes. If using individual shells or ramekins, microwave 4 at a time on high power for 2 minutes. Serves 4 as a main dish.

– Bobii Earle

Curried Scallops

Butter-flavored vegetable cooking
   spray
¾ cup finely shredded carrots
½ cup diced celery
⅛ teaspoon pepper
1 teaspoon margarine
½ pound bay scallops
2 teaspoons dry white wine
¼ teaspoon curry powder
⅛ teaspoon salt
Chopped chives to taste

Spray medium-sized skillet with cooking spray; heat on medium. Add carrots, celery, and pepper. Sauté 1½ minutes until crisp-tender. Remove from skillet to a serving platter and keep warm. Spray the skillet again with cooking spray. Add margarine and place over medium heat. Sauté scallops for 30 seconds. Add wine, curry powder, and salt. Sauté for 1½ minutes more. Place scallops over the vegetables and sprinkle with chives. Serve immediately. Serves 2.

NOTE: A simple variation for a supremely simple and delicious entree.

Glazed Bay Scallops
Wonderfully easy

3 tablespoons margarine or olive
oil or a combination of the two
1 pound bay scallops, washed
2 tablespoons lemon juice
4 tablespoons sherry
1 teaspoon sugar
3 tablespoons fresh minced garlic
4 tablespoons chopped fresh
parsley
Salt and pepper to taste

Heat the margarine or olive oil in a large frying pan. Add the scallops and cook over medium heat just until white, about 2 minutes. Remove scallops from the pan leaving the scallop liquid. Set scallops aside. Immediately add the lemon juice, sherry, and sugar to the scallop liquid and boil until reduced by about half and mixture has turned a golden brown. Add the sautéed scallops, garlic, and parsley and heat through. Serves 2 as a main dish or 4 as an appetizer.

NOTE: Sea scallops can be used in this recipe - cut them into quarters before cooking.

Quick and Easy Shrimp Curry

4 tablespoons butter or margarine
4 tablespoons flour
1 teaspoon salt
Dash pepper
2 cups milk
6 tablespoons catsup
1 to 2 teaspoons curry powder
Dash paprika
1 (12 to 16-ounce) package frozen
cooked shrimp, thawed

Melt butter or margarine in medium size saucepan. Stir in flour, salt, and pepper; cook, stirring constantly, just until bubbling. Stir in milk and continue cooking and stirring until sauce thickens and boils 1 minute. Stir in catsup, curry powder, and paprika, blending well. Add shrimp to sauce and keep over low heat until heated through. Serve over rice. Serves 4.

– Laurie Farquharson

Heath's Cajun Boiled Shrimp

Straight from Bayou country

6 quarts water
1½ cups salt
2 large onions, quartered
1 lemon, halved
1 green pepper, halved
1 whole pod of garlic, halved
2 teaspoons cayenne pepper
1 (3-ounce) box Zatarain's Crab Boil
3 pounds large fresh shrimp

Fill a 10 to 12-quart pot or kettle with water. Add salt, onions, lemon, green pepper, garlic, cayenne, and crab boil. Bring to a hard boil. Add shrimp and when water begins to boil again boil for 2 minutes. Cover pot and remove from the heat. Let sit covered for 20 minutes. Then pour contents of pot into a large colander and immediately add 2-3 handsful of ice. This helps to stop the cooking and cool the shrimp. Peel and serve immediately with favorite dipping sauce. Many people like a sauce made of catsup, horse-radish, fresh lemon juice, salt, and a few drops of Tabasco. Serves 6.

NOTE: This recipe is straight from Bayou country. Don't be alarmed by the large amount of salt called for. It is needed to permeate the shrimps' shells as they are cooking.

–Kathy Heath

Shrimp Scampi

Marvelous

¾ pound medium-sized shrimp, shelled and deveined
6 tablespoons butter or margarine
1 tablespoon minced green onion
1 tablespoon olive oil or vegetable oil
4 to 5 cloves garlic, minced or pressed
2 teaspoons lemon juice
¼ teaspoon salt
2 tablespoons parsley, minced
¼ teaspoon grated lemon peel
Dash of liquid hot pepper seasoning

Pat shrimp dry with paper towels; set aside. Melt butter or margarine in a wide frying pan over medium heat. Stir in green onion, oil, garlic, lemon juice, and salt; cook until bubbly. Add shrimp to pan and cook, stirring occasionally, until shrimp turn pink (4-5 minutes). Stir in parsley, lemon peel, and hot pepper seasoning. Serve immediately. Makes 2 servings.

– Ellen Koenig

Shrimp Creole

An ethnic specialty

½ cup vegetable oil
1 cup chopped green pepper
2 cups chopped onion
1 cup chopped celery
2 tablespoons minced garlic
2 cups tomatoes, peeled, seeded, and chopped
1 tablespoon paprika
¼ teaspoon cayenne
1 teaspoon salt
1 teaspoon white pepper
3 cups water
1 bay leaf
2 tablespoons cornstarch and 2 tablespoons water
3 pounds raw shrimp, peeled and deveined

Heat vegetable oil and sauté next 4 ingredients until tender. Add tomatoes and cook 3-4 more minutes. Stir in paprika, cayenne, salt, pepper, water and bay leaf. Simmer 15 minutes. Add shrimp and continue cooking an additional 15 minutes. Thicken with cornstarch mixed in cold water. Serve with hot fluffy rice. Makes 4-6 servings.

– Gigi Roberts

Shrimp with Vegetables

2 cloves garlic
1 cup firmly packed fresh basil
  leaves (do not substitute dried
  basil)
2 tablespoons grated Parmesan
  cheese
3 tablespoons olive oil
2 tablespoons dry white wine
Salt and pepper to taste
2 carrots, julienned (slices about
  2 inches long and ¼ to ½-inch
  thick)
1 sweet yellow pepper, julienned
1 sweet green pepper, julienned
1 sweet red pepper, julienned
½ pound snow peas, trimmed
2 zucchini, julienned
Juice of 1 lemon
⅓ cup dry white wine
1½ pounds fresh shrimp, peeled
  and deveined

With motor running, drop garlic cloves through the feeder tube of a food processor or blender. Stop the motor and add the basil and Parmesan cheese. Cover and process until the mixture is chopped. With the motor running, drizzle 1 tablespoon of the oil and 2 tablespoons wine through the feed tube. Add salt and pepper to taste. Heat the remaining 2 tablespoons oil in a large skillet over moderate heat. Stir-fry the carrots 3 minutes. Add the pepper strips, snow peas, and zucchini. Stir-fry another 2 minutes or until vegetables are crisply tender. Sprinkle with the lemon juice. Season with salt and pepper. Meanwhile, simmer the ⅓ cup wine in a skillet over moderate heat. Add the shrimp and cover. Simmer gently for 3 minutes or just until the shrimp are cooked. Add the basil mixture. Toss briefly over low heat until the mixture is just heated through. Combine the shrimp mixture with the vegetables. May be served over linguini or spaghetti. Makes 6 servings.

–Marzia Vitali

PASTA AND RICE

Garlic and Clam Sauce for Pasta

Extremely tasty without loads of butter

½ cup chopped onion
½ cup chopped green pepper
2 teaspoons prepared minced
  garlic or 4 cloves garlic, minced
3 tablespoons olive oil
½ pound sliced mushrooms
2 (6½-ounce) cans chopped clams,
  undrained
1½ teaspoons dried thyme
2 tablespoons chopped fresh
  parsley
Dash cayenne pepper
Salt to taste
Freshly ground black pepper
  to taste
8 ounces uncooked spaghetti
  or angel hair pasta cooked
  according to package directions

In a large frying pan, sauté the onion, green pepper, and garlic in the olive oil until soft but not browned. Add the mushrooms and continue cooking over medium heat until they just begin to wilt, about 5 minutes. Add all other ingredients and cook until heated through, about another 5 minutes. Serve over hot cooked spaghetti or angel hair pasta. Serves 3-4.

NOTE: This is an extremely tasty, lower calorie version of the typical white clam sauce that uses butter. Try it and see.

Red Clam Sauce for Pasta
The best you'll ever taste

1 medium onion, chopped
½ teaspoon prepared minced
  garlic
2 tablespoons olive oil
1 (16-ounce) can tomatoes,
  crushed
1 (10¾-ounce) can (1¼ cups)
  tomato puree
¼ teaspoon salt
3 drops Tabasco sauce
Black pepper to taste
1 bay leaf
½ teaspoon oregano
1 (7½-ounce) can chopped clams,
  drained
1 (7½-ounce) can chopped clams,
  undrained
1 pound dried spaghetti, cooked
  and drained

Sauté the onion and garlic in oil until softened. Add the tomatoes, tomato puree, salt, Tabasco, black pepper, bay leaf and oregano. Simmer, covered, for 30 minutes. Just before serving add the drained and undrained clams and heat through. Serve over hot cooked spaghetti. Serves 4-6.

Easy Tomato Vegetable Sauce for Pasta

1 medium carrot
1 medium onion
1 large stalk celery
1 teaspoon prepared minced garlic
3 tablespoons olive oil
1 (16-ounce) can tomatoes,
  crushed
1 teaspoon dried basil
Salt and pepper to taste
1 pound rotelle pasta, cooked and
  drained

Place carrot, onion, celery, and garlic in food processor and chop finely. Heat olive oil in a large skillet. Sauté chopped vegetables in oil for 10 minutes. Add tomatoes, basil, salt and pepper and simmer, covered, for 30 minutes. Serve over hot cooked pasta. Serves 4.

NOTE: A sauce that is also good with cheese - or - meat-filled ravioli.

Salsa Picante for Pasta

No one notices lack of meat

½ cup olive oil
¼ cup wine vinegar
¼ cup tomato puree
2 green onions, finely chopped
1 garlic clove, chopped
2 tablespoons minced fresh
  parsley
Salt and pepper to taste
1 pound pasta, cooked

Combine the olive oil and vinegar in a medium bowl. Add the tomato puree and mix well. Whisk in the onion, garlic, parsley, salt and pepper, blending well. Let the sauce stand at room temperature for 1 hour. Combine with 1 pound of your choice of cooked pasta and serve. Makes 4 servings.

NOTE: This is a wonderful hot weather meal. All you have to cook is the pasta. Serve with a salad.

Chicken Filled Shells

Perfect to make on a cold winter afternoon

2 cups cubed cooked chicken
1 cup cooked peas
½ cup mayonnaise
2 small tomatoes, chopped
¼ cup Parmesan cheese
¼ teaspoon garlic powder
1 (10¾-ounce) can cream of
  mushroom soup
¾ soup can milk
1 (12-ounce) package jumbo pasta
  shells, cooked and drained

Mix together the first 6 ingredients. Combine the soup and milk and stir ¼ of the mixture into the chicken mixture. Stuff the shells with the chicken mixture; arrange in a single layer in a 13x9-inch baking dish. Pour the remaining soup mixture over the shells. Cover with foil. Bake at 325°F for 25 minutes. Garnish with parsley, if desired. Serves 8.

– Judy Booth

Lazy Day Overnight Lasagna
Exceptionally easy

1 pound ground beef
1 (32-ounce) jar prepared
  spaghetti sauce
1 cup water
1 (15-ounce) carton ricotta cheese
2 tablespoons chopped chives
½ teaspoon oregano leaves
1 egg, beaten
8 ounces *uncooked* lasagna
  noodles
1 (12-ounce) package shredded or
  sliced Mozzarella cheese
2 tablespoons Parmesan cheese

Brown the beef in a large skillet; drain well. Add the spaghetti sauce and water; blend well. Simmer for 5 minutes. In a medium bowl, combine the Ricotta cheese, chives, oregano, and egg and mix together well. In the bottom of a 13x9-inch baking dish spread 1½ cups of the meat sauce. Top with ½ of the uncooked noodles, ½ of the Ricotta cheese mixture, and ½ of the Mozzarella cheese. Repeat. Top with the remaining meat sauce and sprinkle with the Parmesan cheese. Cover and refrigerate *overnight*. Bake uncovered at 350°F for 50-60 minutes and let stand for 15 minutes before serving. Serves 8.

– Becky Dunn

Spinach Noodle Bake
Two for one entree

2 (10½-ounce) packages frozen
  chopped spinach, thawed and
  drained
1 pound ziti noodles, cooked and
  drained
1 pound ricotta cheese
2 (15½-ounce) jars marinara sauce
3 eggs, lightly beaten
⅔ cup grated Parmesan cheese
⅓ cup chopped fresh parsley
2 teaspoons salt
½ teaspoon freshly ground pepper

Preheat oven to 350°F. Combine all ingredients in a large mixing bowl and blend thoroughly. Place in a lightly greased 3-quart baking dish and bake for 25-30 minutes or until the top is brown and the sauce is bubbly. Makes 8 servings.

NOTE: This can be put into 2 smaller dishes; freeze one for later use. Remove from freezer and add 10-15 minutes to the baking time.

Baked Spaghetti

Only 298 calories per serving

1 (11½-ounce) can tomato juice
1 (14½-ounce) can stewed
tomatoes
1 small onion, minced
¼ pound fresh mushrooms, sliced
½ sweet red pepper, chopped
1 medium green pepper, chopped
½ teaspoon dried Italian
seasoning
Dash garlic powder
Salt and pepper to taste
1 (8-ounce) box uncooked
spaghetti
1 (4-ounce) package (1 cup)
part-skim grated Mozzarella
cheese
4 teaspoons grated Parmesan
cheese

Make a marinara sauce by combining the first 9 ingredients in a heavy saucepan and simmering for 45 minutes. Meanwhile cook the spaghetti according to package directions. Mix the cooked spaghetti and marinara sauce together and place in a lightly greased 8x8-inch square baking dish. Top with Mozzarella cheese. Bake at 325°F for 20-30 minutes or until bubbly. Remove from oven and sprinkle with the Parmesan cheese. Serves 4.

NOTE: A spaghetti dish that is really tasty and low in calories too. You can make the marinara sauce ahead and freeze. Thaw before proceeding with the recipe.

– Joan Murray

Taglierini
Microwavable

2 medium onions, chopped
2 tablespoons vegetable or olive oil
1 pound ground beef
1 bay leaf
½ teaspoon Italian seasoning
1 (28-ounce) can crushed tomatoes
1 (12-ounce) can tomato paste
1 (10-ounce) package frozen chopped spinach
1 (8-ounce) box elbow macaroni
½ cup grated Parmesan cheese
½ cup grated Cheddar cheese

Brown onions in oil. Add ground beef and cook until brown. Add bay leaf, Italian seasoning, crushed tomatoes and tomato paste. Simmer ½ hour with the lid on and ½ hour with the lid off. While the meat sauce is cooking, cook the spinach according to package directions; drain and reserve. Cook the macaroni according to package directions; drain and reserve. Combine the spinach, noodles, and Parmesan cheese. Mix well and place in a greased 2-quart casserole dish. Top with the Cheddar cheese. Bake at 350°F for 15 minutes or in a microwave oven on high for 5 minutes. Serves 6-8.

– Roxanne Johnson

Anytime Pasta
No cook sauce

1½ pounds ripe tomatoes, cut into pieces
½ cup sliced black olives
1 teaspoon chopped garlic
¼ teaspoon salt
¼ teaspoon crushed red pepper
⅛ teaspoon black pepper
⅓ cup olive oil
2 tablespoons pesto sauce
1 pound pasta twists, cooked, either hot or cold

Mix together the tomatoes, olives, garlic, salt, and red and black peppers. Toss with the olive oil. Let this mixture stand for 1 hour at room temperature and then mix with either the hot or cold cooked pasta. Makes 8 servings.

Mexican Macaroni
Invented by a creative cook in a big hurry

3 cups dry macaroni noodles
2 teaspoons margarine or
   vegetable oil
8 ounces Mild Mexican Cheez
   Whiz
1 (2-ounce) jar pimientos

Cook macaroni according to package directions. Drain. Add margarine and Cheez Whiz to macaroni. Place in serving dish. Sprinkle top with chopped pimientos and serve. Makes 4 servings.

– Beth Dover

Stir-Fry Noodles with Bok Choy and Tofu
Fast family dinner

1 (8-ounce) package Japanese
   noodles or vermicelli, cooked
   according to package directions
3 tablespoons vegetable oil
1½ teaspoons minced garlic
1 teaspoon grated fresh ginger
3 cups shredded bok choy
1 cup sliced mushrooms
½ pound cubed tofu
¼ pound julienned cooked ham
2 tablespoons chicken broth
1½ tablespoons soy sauce
Salt and pepper to taste

Toss the cooked noodles with 1 tablespoon of the oil. Heat the remaining oil in a wok or large skillet over medium heat. Add garlic and ginger and stir-fry 30 seconds. Add bok choy and mushrooms and stir-fry until tender-crisp, about 2-3 minutes. Gently fold in tofu and ham. Add noodles, broth, soy sauce, and salt and pepper. Toss to combine. Makes 6 servings.

Garlic Rice Pilaf

1 stick margarine
1 (10¾-ounce) can beef consomme
1 (6-ounce) can sliced
   mushrooms, undrained
1 cup uncooked long grain rice
1 teaspoon garlic powder

In a 1-quart oven-proof dish, heat the butter and consomme over low heat until the butter melts. Add the mushrooms (including their liquid), rice, and garlic powder; stir to mix well and cover. Place in a 350°F oven and bake for 1 hour. Serves 4.

– Marian Johnson

Pineapple Pilaf

Perks up ham or chicken dishes

1 (20-ounce) can pineapple
  chunks in syrup
2 cups water
1 cup long grain brown rice
½ teaspoon rosemary
2 tablespoons butter
2 tablespoons soy sauce
1 teaspoon grated fresh ginger
  root
1 tablespoon chopped green onion
¼ cup toasted slivered almonds

Drain pineapple syrup into sauce-pan. Add water and bring to a boil. Stir in rice and rosemary. Cover and simmer 35-40 minutes until liquid is absorbed and rice is done. Stir in pineapple chunks and other remaining ingredients and continue cooking until just heated through. Makes 6 servings.

– Esther Treese

Baked Wild Rice

Make early in the day and pop into oven later

1 (6-ounce) box Uncle Ben's Long
  Grain & Wild Rice
¼ cup wild rice
1 medium onion, chopped
½ pound mushrooms, sliced
1 (4-ounce) can water chestnuts,
  drained
¼ cup butter
1 (10¾-ounce) can beef consomme
1 cup burgundy

Pour Uncle Ben's rice into greased casserole. Wash and drain wild rice; add to casserole. Sauté onions, mushrooms, and water chestnuts. Add to rice mixture. Stir in consomme and wine. Cover tightly with foil. Bake at 325°F for 1 hour and 20 minutes. Serves 10.

NOTE: Mix ingredients early in the day and pop into the oven later for baking.

– Susan Scott

Paella

12 small clams in shells
8 ounces chorizo or Italian
  sausage links
1 (2½ to 3 pound) chicken, cut up
1 medium onion, chopped
1 medium green pepper, chopped
1 stalk celery with leaves,
  chopped
2 cloves garlic, minced
1 cup long grain rice
2 large tomatoes, peeled and
  chopped
1 bay leaf
1½ teaspoons salt
½ teaspoon dried oregano,
  crushed
¼ teaspoon thread saffron,
  crushed
2 cups water
12 ounces fresh or frozen shelled
  shrimp
1 (10-ounce) package frozen peas

Cover clams in shells with salted
water using 3 tablespoons salt to 8
cups cold water; let stand 15 minutes. Rinse. Repeat soaking and
rinsing twice.

Cut sausage into 1-inch pieces.
Heat wok over medium high heat.
Add sausage; stir-fry until brown on
both sides. Remove sausage, reserving drippings in wok. Brown chicken
in drippings for about 10 minutes,
turning often. Remove chicken from
wok, reserving drippings.

Stir-fry onions, green peppers,
celery and garlic for about 5 minutes or until onion is tender. Stir in
uncooked rice, tomatoes, bay leaf,
salt, oregano, and saffron; stir-fry 1
minute. Add chicken and water;
cover and simmer 20 minutes, stirring once. Add shrimp, peas, clams,
and cooked sausage. Cover and
simmer about 15 minutes or until
clams open and chicken and rice are
done. Serves 8.

– Cindi Steffens

VEGETABLES

Artichoke and Spinach Casserole

A great party dish

1 (10-ounce) package frozen
chopped spinach
1 (8½-ounce) can artichoke hearts,
drained
1 clove garlic, minced
¼ cup salad oil
¼ cup red wine vinegar
2 tablespoons butter
2 tablespoons all purpose flour
1 cup half and half
½ cup freshly grated Parmesan
cheese
Salt and pepper to taste
⅛ cup freshly grated Parmesan
cheese

Preheat oven to 350°F. Cook spinach according to package directions; drain. Combine oil, vinegar and garlic and pour over the artichokes. Melt butter and stir in flour. Gradually add half and half, stirring constantly with a wire whisk. Add ½ cup Parmesan cheese. Add spinach, salt and pepper. Remove artichokes from marinade and place in bottom of a small buttered casserole dish. Cover with spinach mixture. Sprinkle with ⅛ cup Parmesan cheese. Bake uncovered for 20 minutes. Makes 4 servings.

– Carolyn Nelson

Cold Asparagus in Mustard Cream

Elegant

2 pounds fresh asparagus
3 egg yolks
2 tablespoons lemon juice
¼ cup Dijon mustard
½ cup olive oil
Salt to taste
Freshly ground black pepper

Prepare the asparagus as follows. Break off and discard the bottom of each stalk at the point where it snaps off most easily. Peel the stalks with a vegetable peeler, removing the scales and stringy skin, but stopping at least an inch from the tips. Fill a large, deep, skillet halfway with water and bring to a boil. Place stalks loosely in the pan and allow the water to return to a boil. Reduce the heat and simmer 3-5 minutes and then place the pan under cold running water until the stalks are cool to the touch. Drain on paper towels and then cover and chill.

Make *Mustard Cream* as follows. With an electric mixer, beat the egg yolks with the lemon juice and mustard for 4 minutes on medium speed. On low speed, slowly add the olive oil, beginning by adding 1 tablespoon at a time, then drizzling the oil in as you beat. Add salt and pepper to taste. Chill thoroughly and serve over cold asparagus. Serves 4 as a vegetable or a salad.

– Connie Cavett

Broccoli Casserole

2 (10-ounce) packages chopped
  broccoli, cooked and drained
1 (10¾-ounce) can cream of
  mushroom soup
2 eggs, beaten
¾ cup mayonnaise
1 small onion, chopped
1 cup grated Cheddar cheese
Salt and pepper to taste
½ (8-ounce) package Ritz crackers
  (one stack), crushed
5 tablespoons butter, melted

Mix all ingredients together. Pour
into a 1-quart greased casserole.
Cover with crackers and drizzle with
melted butter. Bake at 350°F for 45
minutes. Serves 6-8.

– Susan Scott

Broccoli and Rice Casserole

A winner anytime

2 to 3 tablespoons vegetable oil
⅔ cup diced onions
1 (10-ounce) package frozen
  chopped broccoli, thawed
1 (10¾-ounce) can cream of
  chicken soup
½ soup can milk
1 cup water
1 cup minute rice
1 (8-ounce) jar Cheez Whiz
Paprika
2 cups Ritz cracker crumbs
2 tablespoons margarine

Heat oil in large skillet. Add onion
and sauté until tender. Add broccoli
and cook, covered, over low heat for
10 minutes. Add soup, milk, water,
rice, and Cheez Whiz and mix well.
Bring to a boil, stirring constantly.
Pour into a buttered 1½-quart casserole dish. Bake at 350°F for 15
minutes.

Sauté the cracker crumbs in the
margarine. Spread over the casserole and bake for another 10
minutes. Serves 6.

– Gail Loeffler

Broccoli with Sesame Cumin Butter

A Presidential treat

1 (10-ounce) package frozen
   broccoli
2 teaspoons sesame seeds
1½ tablespoons margarine
¾ teaspoon ground cumin
Salt to taste
Fresh lemon juice to taste

Cook the broccoli according to package directions. Meanwhile, toast the sesame seeds in a heavy skillet over moderate heat until golden. Add the margarine, cumin and salt. Heat and stir. Pour over the cooked broccoli and sprinkle with lemon juice. Serves 2-4.

NOTE: By now we all know that broccoli is the most nutritious vegetable we can eat. However, if you're getting bored with eating it the same old way, try this delightful variation.

Saucy Brussels Sprouts

2 (10-ounce) packages frozen
   brussels sprouts
½ cup chopped onion
2 tablespoons butter
1 tablespoon flour
1 tablespoon brown sugar
1 teaspoon salt
½ teaspoon dry mustard
½ cup milk
1 cup sour cream
1 tablespoon parsley

Cook brussels sprouts as directed; drain. Cook onion in butter until tender but not brown. Stir in flour, brown sugar, salt, and dry mustard until blended. Stir in milk and cook until thick and bubbly. Blend in sour cream and cook until hot but do not boil. Add brussels sprouts and parsley and mix gently. Serves 6-8.

– Kathy Reynolds

"Bright Eyed" Carrots

From the family that grows "Bright Eye" carrots

2 pounds fresh carrots (preferably
  "Bright Eyes"), sliced
1 cup sugar
1 stick butter
Pinch salt

Place all ingredients into a saucepan. Do *not* add water. Cover saucepan tightly and cook on medium heat for 5 minutes. Turn down to low and continue cooking until done - about 1 hour. Serves 8.

NOTE: The Clonts are farmers and raise "Bright Eyes" carrots. These candied carrots are a nice alternative to candied sweet potatoes for holiday meals.

– Thelma Clonts

Carrot Casserole

2 (16-ounce) bags frozen sliced
  carrots
2 medium onions, chopped
4 tablespoons butter
1 (10¾-ounce) can cream of
  mushroom soup
Salt and pepper to taste
⅓ cup bread crumbs
⅓ cup grated mild Cheddar cheese

Cook carrots until very tender; drain and mash. Sauté onions in butter until golden. Combine mashed carrots, onions, cream of mushroom soup, and salt and pepper and put into a 1-quart baking dish. Sprinkle with bread crumbs and cheese. Bake at 350°F for 25 minutes. Serves 8.

– Susan Scott

Carrot Cinnamon Casserole

A colorful holiday casserole

2 cups mashed cooked carrots
  (about 1 pound raw carrots)
1 stick butter, melted
½ cup white sugar
½ cup brown sugar
3 tablespoons flour
1 teaspoon baking powder
3 eggs, well beaten
½ teaspoon cinnamon

Put carrots into a mixing bowl; add remaining ingredients one at a time and mix well. Transfer to a 1-quart baking dish. Bake at 400°F for 15 minutes. Lower heat to 350°F and continue to bake for 45 minutes. Serve immediately. Makes 6 servings.

– Marian Johnson

Carrots and Celery with Cumin

A magical combination

1 pound carrots, scraped
2 ribs celery with top leaves
½ cup water
Salt to taste
2 tablespoons butter
¼ teaspoon ground cumin

Cut the carrots into very thin slices - there should be about 3½ cups. Set aside. Cut away the top leaves of the celery; chop and set aside. Trim the celery stalks and cut into small cubes - there should be about ½ cup. Set aside. Put the carrots into a saucepan and add the water. Bring to a boil and cover tightly. Cook 5 minutes until most of the water has evaporated. Add the salt, butter, cumin and celery cubes. Stir and cover; cook about 1 minute and remove from the heat. Sprinkle the carrots and celery with the chopped celery leaves and stir. Serve at once. Serves 4.

Joan's Jumpback Eggplant

1 medium eggplant, cubed
2 large zucchini, cubed
1 yellow pepper, chopped
1 red pepper, chopped
1 large onion, chopped
3 large cloves garlic, chopped
¼ cup olive oil
¾ pound feta cheese
Pepper to taste
1 large tomato, cut into chunks

Sauté all vegetables except tomato in olive oil until just tender, about 10 minutes. Crumble feta cheese over the top. Sprinkle with pepper. Stir tomato chunks into vegetable mixture. Cover and continue cooking until heated through, about 5 minutes. Serves 4.

Mom Sellers' Eggplant Fritters

Will turn you into an eggplant lover

1 small eggplant
½ cup flour
2 teaspoons baking powder
½ teaspoon salt
1 egg

Peel and dice the eggplant. Boil in water to cover (use as little water as possible) until tender. Drain and mash. Add the flour, baking powder and salt to the eggplant and mix well. Beat the egg and add to the eggplant mixture. Drop by teaspoonsful into hot oil. Drain on paper towels. Serve immediately. Serves 4.

– Sue Kincaid

Mushrooms Florentine

1 pound fresh mushrooms, sliced thickly
3 tablespoons margarine, melted
½ teaspoon prepared minced garlic, optional
4 green onions, tops included, chopped
¼ cup margarine, melted
2 (10-ounce) packages frozen spinach, cooked and squeezed dry
½ cup grated Colby cheese
½ cup grated Swiss cheese

Sauté the mushrooms in 3 tablespoons margarine. Add the optional garlic if you wish. Sauté the green onions in ¼ cup margarine; add the spinach. Line an 8½x8½-inch pan with the spinach, making some go up the sides. Pour the mushrooms in on top of the spinach. Combine the Colby and Swiss cheeses and sprinkle on top of the mushrooms. Bake at 350°F for 20 minutes. Makes 6 servings.

– Susan Scott

Old Fashioned Baked Pineapple

Ham companion

1 (28-ounce) can pineapple rings, drained and syrup reserved
¼ stick margarine, melted
1 cup sugar
½ cup flour
Salt to taste

Make a sauce of the reserved pineapple juice, margarine, sugar, flour, and salt. Place pineapple rings in a 13x9x2-inch baking dish. Pour the sauce over the pineapple and bake at 350°F for 30 mintues. Serves 8-10.

Favorite Potatoes

1 (2-pound) bag frozen chunky hash brown potatoes
2 (10¾-ounce) cans cream of chicken soup
1 (16-ounce) container (2 cups) sour cream
1 cup chopped onions
1 cup shredded Cheddar cheese
1 cup corn flakes

Mix the first 5 ingredients together. Pour into a 13x9-inch pan. Cover with corn flakes. Bake, uncovered, at 375°F for 1 hour. Serves 6-8.

– Lynne Turton

Easy Oven Baked Potatoes

As tasty as scalloped potatoes but healthier

6 medium potatoes, peeled and cut into ¼-inch slices
6 medium onions, cut into ¼-inch slices
⅓ cup margarine, melted
¾ teaspoon salt
¼ teaspoon celery seeds
1 clove garlic, minced
¼ teaspoon pepper
¼ teaspoon paprika

Layer the potatoes and onions in a 13x9x2-inch glass baking dish. Combine the next 5 ingredients and drizzle over the potatoes and onions. Cover with aluminum foil and bake at 400°F for 40 minutes. Uncover, sprinkle with paprika, re-cover and bake for 20 more minutes. Serves 6-8.

NOTE: Potatoes can be assembled early in the day. Cover and store in refrigerator until time to bake.

Swiss Potatoes

2 tablespoons butter
¼ cup thinly sliced green onions
1 clove garlic, minced
3 cups milk
Salt and pepper to taste
1 tablespoon flour
6 medium potatoes, peeled and
thinly sliced
1½ cups grated Swiss cheese

Preheat oven to 350°F. Melt butter in large saucepan. Add green onions and garlic. Cook until tender. Add milk and bring to a boil. Add salt, pepper, and flour. Stir until smooth. Drop in potato slices. Return to a boil. Simmer, covered, for 5 minutes. Add ½ cup of the cheese. Stir until blended. Pour into a buttered 13x9-inch casserole dish. Top with remaining cheese. Bake until cheese is brown, about 30 minutes. Makes 10 servings.

– Esther Treese

Baked Spinach Au Gratin
No cheese

3 tablespoons butter or a mixture
of butter and olive oil
2 pounds fresh spinach, finely
chopped and steamed
Salt and pepper to taste
1 clove garlic, minced, optional
¼ cup dry bread crumbs

Preheat oven to 375°F. Butter a flat gratin dish with 1 tablespoon of butter. Arrange the spinach in the dish and season with salt and pepper. Sprinkle with garlic if desired. Spread bread crumbs over the spinach and dot the surface of the spinach with small bits of the remaining butter; if using oil, drizzle over the spinach. Bake for 20-25 minutes until the spinach is tender and the bread crumbs are browned. Serves 4-6.

NOTE: 2 (10-ounce) packages of frozen chopped spinach (cooked and drained) may be substituted for the fresh spinach. While we usually associate "au gratin" with cheese it may simply refer to a light coating of bread crumbs or cracker crumbs.

– Sher Kreisler

Sweet Potato Pone

A delicious alternative to candied sweet potatoes

½ cup milk
2 eggs
¼ cup butter, softened
¾ cup brown sugar
½ teaspoon salt
½ teaspoon ginger
½ teaspoon cinnamon
3 cups diced raw sweet potatoes

Place the ingredients in the order given, in a blender. Blend for one minute; push down and then continue blending until smooth. Pour into a greased 13x9-inch baking dish. Bake at 350°F for 45 minutes (or until firm when you shake it). Slice into squares to serve. Serves 8.

– Edie Fagan

Zucchini or Broccoli Bake

A great cheesy flavor

1½ cups zucchini or broccoli, thinly sliced
1 cup baking mix
½ cup Parmesan cheese
½ cup chopped onion
½ cup vegetable oil
½ cup shredded Mozzarella cheese

Mix zucchini or broccoli, baking mix, Parmesan cheese, onion and oil together. Place in a 9x12-inch pan; sprinkle Mozzarella cheese on top. Bake at 350°F for 25 minutes. Serves 6.

– Lorraine Santy

Zucchini Parmesan

¼ cup margarine
2 medium zucchini, cut in chunks
1 onion, thinly sliced
2 tomatoes, cut in chunks
Salt and pepper to taste
¼ cup water
¼ cup Parmesan cheese
1 tablespoon soy sauce

Melt margarine in frying pan. Add zucchini chunks, sliced onions, tomato chunks, seasonings and water. Cover and cook for 10 minutes. Sprinkle with cheese and soy sauce. Cover and simmer for 25 more minutes. Serves 4

– Susan Scott

Baked Stuffed Zucchini

4 medium zucchini
2 quarts boiling water
⅔ cups baking mix
½ cup shredded Swiss cheese
⅓ cup mayonnaise
1 egg, beaten
2 tablespoons chopped onion
¼ teaspoon salt
¼ teaspoon pepper

Put zucchini in boiling water. Return to a boil. Reduce heat and simmer uncovered for 5 minutes. Drain and cool. Cut each zucchini lengthwise into halves. Scoop out centers, and chop and drain them. Mix chopped zucchini with all other ingredients. Fill zucchini halves. Bake in a dish at 450°F for 20 minutes - until puffy and golden brown. Serves 8.

– Susan Scott

Garden Casserole
Colorful and nutritious

1 tablespoon margarine, melted
2 cups fresh green beans, washed, drained and cut into 1-inch pieces
3 carrots, thinly sliced
1 green pepper, chopped
1 onion, chopped
2 cups sliced celery
1½ teaspoons salt
½ teaspoon pepper
1 tablespoon sugar
2 tablespoons cornstarch
1 (16-ounce) can tomatoes, undrained and chopped
3 tablespoons margarine

Coat a 3-quart glass casserole dish with the melted margarine. Layer the green beans, carrots, green pepper, onion, and celery in the casserole. Combine the salt, pepper, sugar and cornstarch and sprinkle over the vegetables. Top with the tomatoes and dot with the 3 tablespoons of margarine. Bake, uncovered, at 350°F for 1 hour. Makes 10 servings.

Easy Garden Vegetable Pie

2 cups fresh broccoli
Water to measure one inch in
frying pan
½ teaspoon salt
½ cup chopped onion
½ cup chopped green pepper
1 cup (4 ounces) shredded
Cheddar cheese
1½ cups milk
¾ cup baking mix
3 eggs
1 teaspoon salt
¼ teaspoon pepper

Preheat oven to 400°F. Add salt to water to measure one inch in frying pan and bring to a boil. Add broccoli, cover and heat again to boiling. Cook until almost tender, about 5 minutes; drain thoroughly. Mix broccoli, onion, green pepper, and cheese in a lightly greased 10-inch pie plate.

Beat remaining ingredients together for one minute or until smooth. Pour over vegetables in pie plate. Bake for 35-40 minutes or until golden brown and knife inserted in center comes out clean. Let stand 5 minutes before cutting. Makes 8 servings.

– Esther Treese

Slow-Cooked Ratatouille
Crockpot gourmet

4 medium tomatoes
1¾ cups chopped onion
½ teaspoon prepared minced
garlic
2 tablespoons olive oil
2 medium green peppers, cut into
½-inch strips
½ pound eggplant, cut into ½-inch
strips
½ pound zucchini, cut into ½-inch
strips
1 teaspoon dried basil
½ teaspoon dried thyme
1½ teaspoons salt

Peel tomatoes by dropping into boiling water for 10 seconds. Remove from boiling water and peel under cold running water; chop coarsely and reserve. In a large skillet cook the onion and garlic in the olive oil until softened. Transfer this mixture to a crock-pot. Add the tomatoes, peppers, eggplant, zucchini, basil, thyme, and salt to the crock-pot. Cover and cook on high for 3-4 hours. Serve hot. Serves 6-8.

Baked Squash

Perfect side dish for meat, poultry, or fish

3 pounds yellow summer squash, cut into chunks
½ cup chopped onions
1 egg
1 teaspoon salt
½ teaspoon pepper
1 teaspoon lemon juice or grated lemon rind
1 stick butter or margarine
½ cup bread crumbs or cracker meal

Boil squash in boiling water until tender, about 3-5 minutes. Drain thoroughly and mash. Add onions, egg, salt, pepper, lemon juice, and half of the butter. Mash mixture together; pour into 8½x8½-inch baking dish.

Melt remaining butter, spread over squash mixture and sprinkle with cracker meal or bread crumbs. Bake at 375°F for 1 hour or until brown on top. To serve, cut into squares. Makes 6 generous servings.

NOTE: The squash can be made ahead and reheated. Wrap in aluminum foil and reheat at 350°F for 25-30 minutes.

– Bettye S. Smith

EGGS, CHEESE AND BEANS

Egg Soufflé For a Crowd

Serve at your next tennis luncheon

⅓ to ½ cup margarine
16 slices bread, crusts trimmed
1 pound Cheddar cheese,
  shredded
10 eggs
4 cups milk
1 teaspoon dry mustard

Spread margarine on both sides of bread. Layer 8 slices of bread in a 13x9-inch casserole dish and sprinkle with half of the cheese. Make another layer of the remaining bread and cheese. Beat eggs, milk, and dry mustard together and pour over the bread and cheese. Refrigerate overnight. Bake, uncovered, at 300°F for 45 minutes or until a knife comes out clean. Makes 8-10 servings.

– Linda Stevenson

Cheese Soufflé

So easy to make ahead

10 slices white bread, crusts
  removed
4 (5-ounce) jars Old English
  Cheddar Cheese Spread
1 scant (16-ounce) container
  margarine (about ⅔ cup)
4 eggs
1 pint milk
Dash Worcestershire sauce

Cream cheese and margarine together until soft and smooth. Spread mixture on each piece of bread and cut each piece into quarters. Lay each quarter of bread in 13x9-inch glass baking dish. Beat eggs and add milk and Worcestershire and continue mixing until well blended. Pour over the top of the bread. Cover and refrigerate overnight. Bake at 350°F for 1 hour. Serves 6-8.

– Susie Mayer

Spinach and Crab Quiche

Memorable Maine entree

1 (9-inch) deep dish frozen pie
crust
1½ cups grated Gruyere cheese
1 (10-ounce) package frozen
spinach, thawed and hand
squeezed
¾ cup (6 ounces) crab meat,
picked and flaked
4 eggs, lightly beaten
1 tablespoon flour
1½ cups light cream
1 tablespoon minced onion
Pinch of salt
Black pepper to taste

Bake pie crust according to package directions. (If you wish you may fill the crust with dried beans or uncooked rice to keep it flat while baking.) Sprinkle ½ cup of the grated cheese on the bottom of the baked pie shell. Mix spinach and crab together; spread on top of the cheese. Combine the eggs, flour, cream, minced onion, salt, and pepper and the rest of the cheese. Pour this over the spinach/crab filling. Bake at 400°F for 15 minutes and 325°F for 30 minutes or until firm. Serves 6 for luncheon.

NOTE: This recipe was painstakingly reconstructed from memory of a delicious quiche consumed in a Maine restaurant. Numerous experimental recipes were tried before hitting on the right combination of ingredients.

– Cela Johnson

Rancho Baked Beans

1 pound ground beef
2 cups chopped onion
1 teaspoon salt
1 cup ketchup
2 tablespoons prepared mustard
1 tablespoon vinegar
1 cup brown sugar
2 (16-ounce) cans pork and beans
1 (16-ounce) can kidney beans,
  drained
2 tablespoons shortening (not all
  grease from ground beef)

Brown ground beef and onion.
Mix the rest of the ingredients.
Combine cooked ground beef and
onions with rest of ingredients. Bake
at 350°F for 45 minutes. Serves 6.

– Ann McKibbin

Four Bean Bake

Crowd pleaser

1 tablespoon Worcestershire
  sauce
1 tablespoon dry mustard
1 teaspoon salt
3 tablespoons vinegar
½ cup catsup
½ cup brown sugar
1 (30-ounce) can kidney beans,
  drained
1 (28-ounce) can cut green beans,
  drained
1 (16-ounce) can baby lima beans,
  drained
2 (28-ounce) cans B & M beans,
  undrained and pork slices
  removed
6 slices raw bacon

Mix Worcestershire sauce, dry
mustard, salt, vinegar, catsup, and
brown sugar together in a saucepan.
Heat until the sugar is dissolved.
Mix the sauce and all of the beans
together and put into a heavy
3-quart casserole. Dice 6 slices raw
bacon and place on top of the beans.
Bake at 300°F for 1 hour. Serves
10-12.

NOTE: Be prepared - everyone will
ask for this recipe! Beans can be assembled a day ahead if you wish.

– Edie Fagan

Brunch Casserole

1 (6-ounce) box seasoned croutons
1 pound ham, cubed _or_ 1 pound
   bacon, crisply fried and
   crumbled
1½ cups Cheddar cheese
8 eggs
2 cups milk
1 teaspoon mustard
¾ stick margarine, melted

Layer croutons, ham, and cheese. Beat eggs, milk and mustard and pour over the other ingredients. Drizzle the melted butter over the top. Cover with foil and refrigerate overnight. Bake at 350°F for 45 minutes, covered and 15 minutes, uncovered. Cool for 10 minutes and then cut into squares. Makes 6-8 servings.

– Sherry Lorenzen

Cheese Quiche

1 pound Monterey Jack cheese
   with jalapenos
1 pound sharp Cheddar cheese
1 (4-ounce) can chopped green
   chilies, drained (optional)
6 eggs
1 (13-ounce) can evaporated milk

Grate cheeses into lasagna pan. If using green chilies, spread over the cheeses at this time. Beat eggs and evaporated milk together and pour over cheese mixture. Bake at 375°F for 40 minutes. This may be served hot or cold. Makes 6-8 servings.

– Shirley Clark

"Cheesy" Easy Quiche

8 eggs
½ cup flour
1 teaspoon baking powder
¾ teaspoon salt
4 cups (1 pound) shredded
   Monterey jack cheese or 2 cups
   jack cheese and 2 cups Cheddar
   cheese
1½ cups cottage cheese
¼ cup chopped bell pepper or 1
   (4-ounce) can chopped chilies

Beat eggs 3 minutes. Combine flour, baking powder, and salt. Mix well. Stir in cheeses and pepper or chilies. Pour in a greased 13x9-inch pan. (For higher quiche, use 11x7-inch pan.) Bake at 350°F for 35-40 minutes. Cool before cutting into squares. Serves 8-10.

NOTE: You can have great snacks on hand by making this quiche and freezing. Cut into squares and wrap individually before placing in freezer. Unwrap and warm quiche squares in microwave.

– Gale P. Grimm

Midnight Eggs

½ cup margarine
1 teaspoon salt
Pepper to taste
½ cup milk
1 (8-ounce) package cream
   cheese, diced
24 eggs

Melt margarine; add salt, pepper, salt, milk, and cheese. Beat eggs. Combine eggs and cheese mixture. Place in a 13x9-inch casserole dish. Place dish in pan of water in oven. Bake at 300°F for 1 hour. Allow to cool a few minutes before serving. Serves 15-18.

Black-Eyed Pea Casserole

1 (10-ounce) bag frozen black-eyed
  peas
1 cup diced ham
1 (16-ounce) can tomatoes
¼ cup chopped onion
¼ cup chopped green pepper
1 cup cooked white rice
Pepper to taste

Cook the peas according to package directions. When done, mix with the ham, tomatoes, onion, green pepper, cooked rice, and black pepper. Pour into a lightly greased 3-quart casserole and bake at 350°F for 45 minutes. Serves 4.

NOTE: Easy and nutritious. Start early so the beans will be thoroughly cooked.

Easy Black-Eyed Pea Skillet Dinner
Happy New Year

1 large onion, chopped
1 medium green pepper, chopped
2 tablespoons margarine
1 pound ground round or other
  low-fat ground beef
1 (16-ounce) can tomatoes,
  undrained and crushed
2 (16-ounce) cans black-eyed peas,
  drained
1 teaspoon salt
½ teaspoon pepper
2 cups hot cooked white rice

In a large skillet, sauté the onion and green pepper in margarine until soft but not browned. Add ground round and continue cooking until meat is browned. Drain any grease that has appeared. Add tomatoes, black-eyed peas, salt, and pepper. Bring mixture to a boil, reduce heat and simmer, uncovered, for 30 minutes. Serve over hot cooked rice. Makes 6 servings.

Lentils, Monastery Style
Vegetarian main dish

1 large onion, chopped
1 carrot, chopped
¼ cup olive oil
½ teaspoon dried thyme
½ teaspoon marjoram leaves
3 cups vegetable stock (can be made from vegetable boullion cubes)
1 cup dry lentils, washed
Salt to taste
¼ cup chopped parsley
1 (16-ounce) can tomatoes
¼ cup sherry

In a large pot, sauté the onion and carrot in the olive oil for 3-5 minutes. Add the thyme and marjoram and sauté 1 minute more. Add the stock, lentils, salt, parsley, and tomatoes. Cover the pot and simmer until the lentils are tender - about 45 minutes. Add ¼ cup sherry and heat through. Serves 4.

NOTE: Delicious served with corn muffins.

– Joanne Ehrlich

Grandstand Grits
Nice change from potatoes

½ cup quick-cooking grits
1 clove garlic, lightly crushed
⅛ teaspoon pepper
2 cups boiling chicken broth
2 green onions, chopped
1 tablespoon margarine

Stir the first three ingredients into the boiling chicken broth in a medium saucepan. Cook, stirring occasionally, over medium heat until thick, 3-4 minutes. Discard garlic. Stir in onion and margarine. Cover and let stand 5 minutes. Serves 4 as a side dish.

SAUCES

Fat-Free White Sauce Mix
Secret of the guilt free gourmet

2 cups non-fat dry powdered milk
¾ cup cornstarch
¼ cup chicken bouillon powder
4 teaspoons onion powder
1 teaspoon dried thyme
1 teaspoon dried basil
½ teaspoon freshly ground white
    pepper

In a medium-size bowl, stir together all the ingredients. Store in a tightly covered container at room temperature. To use, stir ¼ cup of mix into 1 cup of liquid (such as skim milk or chicken broth, or water). Stir until smooth. If you wish add 1 tablespoon liquid margarine and blend. Heat mixture until thickened. Makes 3 cups dry mix or enough for 12 cups reconstituted white sauce.

NOTE: A miracle recipe. It is very versatile and can be used anytime a white sauce is called for in casseroles, pastas, gravies, etc. Each serving has only 50 calories and none of the high cholesterol ingredients of most white sauces. For variation add any of the following to each cup of sauce:

½ cup grated Parmesan, Cheddar or
    Swiss cheese
½ cup grated cucumber
2 tablespoons dry sherry
1 teaspoon fresh dill or ½ teaspoon
    dried dill
½ teaspoon curry powder
⅓ cup horseradish and ¼ teaspoon
    dry mustard

Beautiful Bearnaise Sauce

Accompanies your favorite roast or steak

1 cup butter
4 egg yolks
2 tablespoons fresh lemon juice
¼ teaspoon salt
¼ teaspoon Tabasco sauce
¼ cup white wine
2 tablespoons tarragon vinegar
1 teaspoon dried tarragon
1 tablespoon chopped shallots
¼ teaspoon freshly ground pepper

In a small pan, heat butter until very hot but not brown. (You may heat in a microwave oven.) Put egg yolks, lemon juice, salt, and Tabasco sauce into a blender. Cover and turn on low speed. Immediately remove blender's small cover and pour in hot butter in a slow steady stream. When the butter is completely added, turn off the blender.

In a small saucepan, combine white wine, tarragon vinegar, tarragon, shallots, and pepper. Bring to a boil and cook rapidly until the liquid is reduced to 2 tablespoons or less. Pour the white wine mixture into the blender with the butter mixture and blend on high speed for about 8 seconds. Makes about 1½ cups.

– Gigi Roberts

Lemon Butter

Keep handy in refrigerator

5 tablespoons lemon juice
¼ pound margarine (1 stick) or
   8 tablespoons

Heat together. Serve over fish or vegetables. Makes ¾ cup.

SAUCES

124

Wine Butter
Perk up veggies

2 tablespoons dry white wine
2 teaspoons white wine vinegar
2 teaspoons minced shallots
4 tablespoons margarine or butter

Combine the first 3 ingredients in a small skillet. Boil down to half of the original mixture. Whisk in margarine. Pour over hot vegetables. Makes ¾ cup.

Lemon Caper Sauce
For both vegetables and seafood

¾ cup olive oil
⅓ cup lemon juice
2 tablespoons capers, drained
¼ teaspoon tarragon
3 cornichons or small gherkins, drained and minced
Salt and pepper to taste

Combine the oil and lemon juice. Beat with a whisk; add the rest of the ingredients while whisking. Pour into a jar and chill. Makes 1¼ cups.

Doc's Mustard Sauce
Magic for meat

4 ounces (1 stick) margarine
5 tablespoons lemon juice (about 2 lemons)
4 tablespoons prepared mustard
4 tablespoons brown sugar
1 tablespoon black pepper
1 tablespoon salt

Melt the margarine in a small saucepan. Add the remaining ingredients. Heat to a low boil stirring continuously. Let cool. Spread over pork, lamb chops, or chicken before grilling or broiling. Keeps well in refrigerator for 1 week. Reheat before using. Makes about 1 cup.

Elegant Raspberry Sauce

Impress your dinner guests

1 (16-ounce) package frozen red
　　raspberries, thawed
1 teaspoon cornstarch
1 tablespoon water
½ cup red currant jelly
¼ cup sugar
4 tablespoons Cointreau or Grand
　　Marnier

Strain the raspberries. Mix the cornstarch and water together and add to the berries; simmer for 5 minutes. Add the jelly and sugar and heat until thoroughly dissolved. Add the Cointreau or Grand Marnier. Chill and store in refrigerator. Makes 6 servings.

NOTE: Serve over fruit - especially peaches or cantaloupe - for a refreshing dessert. Sauce is also wonderful over ice cream or frozen yogurt.

Sherry Sauce

Great gingerbread topper

½ cup cream sherry
1 cup water
2 tablespoons lemon juice
¾ cup brown sugar
½ teaspoon ground cinnamon
1 tablespoon cornstarch
Dash salt
1 tablespoon butter or margarine

Combine first 7 ingredients in a small saucepan and bring to a boil. Reduce heat and simmer for 5-10 minutes, stirring occasionally. When mixture is thick and clear, add butter and melt. Serve warm over pies, gingerbread, ice cream, etc. Serves 8.

CAKES

Apricot Cake

1 box lemon supreme cake mix
4 eggs
¾ cup vegetable oil
1 cup apricot nectar
Juice of 1 lemon
1 cup confectioners sugar

Mix cake mix, eggs, vegetable oil, and apricot nectar together until well blended. Pour into 10-inch bundt or tube pan. Bake at 325°F for 45-50 minutes. Mix and heat lemon juice and confectioners sugar. Frost the cake while it is still warm. Serves 12.

– Marian Johnson

Blueberry Cake
Little effort with big results

1 cup butter, softened
2 cups sugar
4 eggs
1 teaspoon vanilla
3 cups flour
½ teaspoon salt
1 teaspoon baking powder
1 pint fresh blueberries or 2 cups canned blueberries, drained

Cream butter and sugar. Add eggs, one at a time, beating after each until fluffy. Add vanilla. Sift dry ingredients together. Reserve 1 cup flour mixture. Add remaining flour to butter mixture; beat well. Dredge berries in reserved flour. Fold gently into batter. Grease a 10-inch tube pan with butter and dust with sugar. Spoon batter into greased and sugared pan. Bake 1½ hours at 350°F. Serves 12.

– Susan Scott

Cherry Ribbon Delight Cake
Ingenious

1 package white cake mix
1 cup boiling water
1 (3-ounce) package cherry
flavored gelatin (may also use
lime or strawberry)
½ cup crushed pineapple, drained,
with juice reserved
½ cup chopped nuts
2 drops lemon juice
1 cup chilled whipping cream
¼ cup confectioners sugar

Bake cake mix in two 9-inch layer pans as directed on package. Remove from pans and cool.

Meanwhile, pour boiling water over gelatin in bowl, stirring until gelatin is dissolved. Stir in fruit juice; chill until slightly thickened but not set. Stir in pineapple, nuts, and lemon juice.

Place two strips of foil (each 2-3 inches wide) in each of the layer pans, extending foil over pan edges. Place a cooled cake layer in each pan, one layer right side up and one layer upside down. Spoon gelatin mixture evenly on the layers; chill until gelatin is firm.

In chilled bowl, beat cream and sugar until stiff. With extending foil strips, lift cakes out of pans; stack layers gelatin side up. Frost side of cake with whipped cream. Refrigerate any leftover cake. Serves 10-12.

NOTE: It's fun to make this cake in holiday-shaped pans with appropriately colored gelatin. For example use lime gelatin and a shamrock pan for St. Patrick's Day.

– Gail Loeffler

Orange Crunch Cake
Company cake

Crunch Layer

1 cup graham cracker crumbs
½ cup firmly packed brown sugar
½ cup chopped walnuts
½ cup margarine, melted

Cake Layers

**1 package pudding-in-the-mix
yellow cake mix**
½ cup water
½ cup orange juice
⅓ cup vegetable oil
3 eggs
2 tablespoons grated orange peel.

Frosting

**1 can ready-to-serve vanilla
frosting**
**1 cup frozen whipped dessert
topping, thawed**
3 tablespoons grated orange peel
1 teaspoon grated lemon peel

Garnish

**1 (11-ounce) can mandarin orange
slices, drained**
Mint leaves

Heat oven to 350°F. Grease and flour two 9-inch round cake pans. Combine crunch layer ingredients until crumbly. Press half of crunch mix into each prepared pan.

Blend cake ingredients until moistened. Beat on high two minutes. Pour batter evenly over crunch layer. Bake at 350°F for 30-35 minutes. Cool 10 minutes and remove from pans. Cool completely.

Beat frosting until fluffy and add thawed whipped dessert topping. Fold in grated orange and lemon peel.

Place one cake layer, crunch side up, on serving plate. Spread with ¼ of the frosting. Top with remaining layer, crunch-side up. Spread top and sides with remaining frosting. Garnish with orange sections and mint leaves. Store any leftovers in refrigerator. Serves 16.

– Dena Anderton

Fresh Peach Cake

½ cup butter
1½ cups brown sugar, firmly
    packed
1 egg
3 cups flour
1 teaspoon baking soda
Dash salt
1 cup buttermilk
2 cups diced fresh peaches or
    1 (2-pound) can sliced peaches,
    drained
¼ cup sugar
1 teaspoon cinnamon
Whipped cream

Cream butter and sugar until fluffy. Beat in egg. Sift together flour, baking soda, and salt. Add to creamed mixture alternately with buttermilk beating until smooth after each addition. Fold in peaches. Pour into greased 13x9-inch pan. Mix sugar and cinnamon together and sprinkle over top of batter. Bake at 350°F for 30-35 minutes. Serve with whipped cream. Serves 12.

– Susan Scott

"Court" Torte

1 (14-ounce) prepared angel food
    cake (if making your own cake
    use a 10-inch tube pan)
½ pint whipping cream, whipped
1 (8-ounce) can crushed
    pineapple, drained

Slice the cake into 3 layers. Fold the drained pineapple into the whipped cream. Assemble the cake by spreading the pineapple/whipped cream mixture between the layers and on top of the cake. Store in refrigerator. Serves 12.

– Joan Kundis

Orange Sherbet Terrine Cake

Easy to make ahead for guests

1 (10-inch) angel food cake
2 cups orange sherbet, softened
½ cup plus 3 tablespoons
  chocolate-flavored syrup
1 tablespoon Kahlua or other
  coffee-flavored liqueur
½ teaspoon grated orange rind
24 orange sections
Orange twists (optional)

Slice off top third of cake, using a serrated knife; set aside. Hollow out bottom portion of cake, leaving a 1½-inch wide cavity, making sure not to cut through bottom of cake; reserve leftover cake for another use.

Pack sherbet into cavity of cake, pressing firmly with back of spoon; top with remaining third of cake. Wrap in heavy-duty plastic wrap, and freeze 8 hours.

Combine syrup, Kahlua, and orange rind; stir well. Cut cake into 12 slices, drizzle each with sauce, and top with orange sections. Garnish with orange twists, if desired. Yield: 12 servings.

Saint Louis Cake

Easy but tastes fancy

1 box yellow cake mix
1 stick margarine, softened
2 eggs
8 ounces cream cheese
2 eggs
1 (16-ounce) box confectioners
  sugar

Mix cake mix, margarine, and eggs together. Press into a 13x9-inch pan. Beat together cream cheese, eggs, and confectioners sugar. Pour over the first layer and bake at 350°F for 35-40 minutes. Makes 12 servings.

– Connie Cavett

Secret Cake

Can be made from beginning to end in 30 minutes

Cake

2 cups plain flour
2 cups sugar
1 stick margarine
¼ cup solid vegetable shortening
3½ teaspoons cocoa
1 cup water
½ cup buttermilk
2 unbeaten eggs
½ teaspoon salt
1 teaspoon vanilla
1 teaspoon baking soda

Frosting

1 stick margarine
3½ teaspoons cocoa
½ cup buttermilk
1 (16-ounce) box confectioners
   sugar
1 teaspoon vanilla
1 cup chopped nuts

Mix flour and sugar well. Bring margarine, shortening, cocoa and water to a boil. Pour boiled ingredients over the sugar and flour. Mix and blend well. Add buttermilk, eggs, salt, vanilla and soda. Mix well. Batter will be thin. Pour into a 11x16x1-inch pan. Bake at 400°F for 20 minutes *ONLY!* Make frosting while cake bakes.

Boil margarine, cocoa and buttermilk until slightly thickened. Remove from heat and add confectioners sugar, vanilla and nuts. Frost cake directly out of oven while both cake and frosting are still hot.

– Ginny Milks
Joan Kundis

Chocolate Grasshopper Cake

Marvelous

1 box German chocolate or devil's
food (pudding-in-the-mix) cake
mix
3 eggs, beaten
1 cup milk
¼ cup brown crème de cacao
¼ cup green crème de menthe
1 tablespoon vegetable oil
1 (16-ounce) box confectioners
sugar, sifted
½ cup margarine, melted
3 tablespoons green crème de
menthe
2 to 3 tablespoons milk

Combine the cake mix, eggs, milk, crème de cacao, crème de menthe, and vegetable oil. Beat for 5 minutes. Pour into a 13x9-inch glass cake pan which has been sprayed with no stick cooking spray. Bake at 350°F for 40-45 minutes or until the cake springs back when touched. Cool completely (25-30 minutes) before frosting. While cake is cooling make the frosting by combining the confectioners sugar, margarine, and crème de menthe; mix until well blended. Add just enough milk to bring the frosting to a spreading consistency. Frost the cake and cut into 3x4-inch rectangles. Makes 12 servings.

Mom's Boiled Spice Cake
with Caramel Frosting
An old fashioned treat

Cake

2 sticks margarine
2 cups water
2 cups white sugar
2 cups raisins
2 teaspoons ground cloves
2 teaspoons cinnamon
1 teaspoon salt
3 cups flour
2 teaspoons baking soda

Frosting

5 tablespoons heavy cream
1 cup brown sugar
1 cup confectioners sugar
5 large marshmallows

To make cake combine all ingredients except flour and baking soda in a large saucepan. Bring to a boil. When mixture has reached boiling remove from heat and cool. When cool add flour and baking soda and mix well. Pour cake batter into a lightly greased 13x9-inch baking pan and bake at 350°F for 20 minutes or until toothpick comes out clean. Cool cake. Make frosting by bringing the cream and brown sugar to a boil. Remove from the heat and add the confectioners sugar and marshmallows. Stir until marshmallows are melted and frosting is the right consistency to spread. Spread over cooled cake. Makes 12 servings.

Plum Nutty Cake

A championship recipe

Cake

2 cups self-rising flour
2 cups sugar
1 teaspoon cloves
½ teaspoon cinnamon
½ teaspoon allspice
½ teaspoon nutmeg
3 eggs
¾ cup oil
2 (4½-ounce) jars baby food plums
   with tapioca
1 cup chopped nuts

Glaze

1 cup confectioners sugar
1 tablespoon butter, melted
1 teaspoon almond extract
2 tablespoons milk

Oil and flour bundt or angel food cake pan. Sift first 6 ingredients together. Add eggs, oil, and plums and beat for 2 minutes. Stir in nuts. Bake at 300°F for 1 hour. Cool cake completely. Mix glaze ingredients and top cooled cake with glaze. Serves 12.

NOTE: This cake has a fruitcake flavor without the use of citron and candied fruits. If you like nuts, use 2 cups.

– Beth Macomber

Pound Cake

An easy family favorite

2 sticks real butter, room
   temperature
½ cup solid vegetable shortening,
   room temperature
2 cups white sugar
5 eggs, room temperature
3 cups all purpose flour
½ teaspoon baking powder
1 cup whole or low-fat milk
1 teaspoon vanilla
½ teaspoon lemon extract
½ teaspoon almond extract

Cream butter, vegetable shortening, and sugar together. Add eggs one at a time and beat well. Sift flour and baking powder together and add to butter mixture, creaming well. Add milk, vanilla, lemon and almond extracts and mix well. Pour batter into a 10-inch tube pan. Bake in oven at 325°F for 90 minutes. Do not open oven door during baking. Serves 12-16.

NOTE: This recipe has stood the test of time. It's exceptional as the base for strawberry shortcake.

– Pam Crowell

COOKIES AND CANDY

Best Brownies

Melt in your mouth variety

**3 (1-ounce) squares semi-sweet
  chocolate**
1 cup margarine
2 cups sugar
4 eggs
2 cups flour
1 tablespoon vanilla extract
1 cup nuts (optional)

Melt chocolate and margarine in a large saucepan. Stir in sugar and remove from heat. Add eggs, one at a time, mixing well after each one. Stir in flour, vanilla, and nuts. Pour into a greased 13x9x2-inch pan. Bake at 350°F for 30 minutes. Cool and frost with *Best Chocolate Frosting*. (See following recipe.) Makes 24-28 brownies.

– Becky Dunn

Best Chocolate Frosting

For Best Chocolate Brownies

1 stick margarine
¼ cup cocoa
6 tablespoons milk
**1 (16-ounce) box 10-X
  confectioners sugar**
1 teaspoon vanilla

In a large saucepan bring the margarine, cocoa, and milk to a boil. Remove from heat and add the confectioners sugar and vanilla. Beat well and spread on cooled *Best Brownies*.

NOTE: Don't relegate this rich frosting to brownie use only. It makes a great topping for any cake or cookie.

– Becky Dunn

German Chocolate Brownies

1 (14-ounce) bag caramels
1 (14-ounce) can evaporated milk
1 package German Chocolate cake mix
1½ sticks margarine
1 (6-ounce) package chocolate chips
1 cup chopped pecans
1 cup flaked coconut (optional)

Melt the caramels with ⅓ cup of the evaporated milk. Mix the cake mix with the rest of the evaporated milk and the margarine. Spread ½ of this batter in a greased 13x9-inch pan. Sprinkle with chocolate chips and pecans and optional coconut. Drizzle the caramel mixture over the chocolate chip/pecan mixture. Spread the last ½ of the batter over the caramel layer. Bake at 350°F for 15-20 minutes. Cool completely and refrigerate until firm. Makes about 48 (2x1-inch) bars.

– Beth Macomber

Peppermint Brownies

1 stick margarine
2 (1-ounce) squares unsweetened chocolate
2 eggs
1 teaspoon vanilla
1 cup sugar
½ cup flour
¼ teaspoon baking powder
¼ teaspoon salt
½ cup chopped pecans

Frosting

2 tablespoons margarine, melted
1 tablespoon heavy cream
1 cup confectioners sugar
¾ teaspoon peppermint extract

Melt the margarine and chocolate. Cool. Add eggs, vanilla, sugar, flour, baking powder, and salt and mix well. Add nuts and pour into a greased 13x9-inch pan. Bake at 350°F for 15 minutes. Cool. Make frosting by combining the 2 tablespoons margarine, cream, sugar, and peppermint extract. Frost the cooled cake. Refrigerate. Makes about 36 squares.

Blonde Brownies

2⅔ cups sifted all purpose flour
2½ teaspoons baking powder
½ teaspoon salt
⅔ cup butter
2¼ cups brown sugar
3 eggs
1 cup chopped pecans
1 cup semi-sweet chocolate chips
(6-ounce package)

Sift together the flour, baking powder, and salt; set aside. Melt the butter in a large saucepan; add brown sugar and blend well. Let cool 15 minutes. Beat eggs in the brown sugar/butter mixture one at a time. Add flour mixture, pecans, and chocolate chips and mix well. Spread into a greased 15x10x1-inch pan. Bake at 350°F for 25-30 minutes. Cut into 2-inch squares. Makes 3 dozen.

– Bonnie Harwell

Chocolate Toffee Squares

1 package saltine crackers (one stack from 2-stack package)
1 cup light brown sugar
1 cup butter
1 (11¾-ounce) package milk chocolate chips
1 cup ground pecans

Preheat oven to 400°F. Line the bottom and sides of a 15x10-inch pan with aluminum foil. Place crackers (not crumbled) side by side on the bottom of the pan. Place brown sugar and butter in saucepan; bring to a simmer and simmer for 3 minutes. Pour mixture quickly over crackers and then bake in preheated oven for 5 minutes. Remove from oven. Sprinkle chocolate chips over all, spreading to cover as they melt. Sprinkle pecans over the top. Cool and cut into squares. Makes about 75 squares.

– Anita Vining

Butter Pecan Turtle Cookies

Crust

2 cups all purpose flour
1 cup firmly packed brown sugar
½ cup butter, softened
1 cup whole pecans

Caramel Layer

½ cup firmly packed brown sugar
⅔ cup butter
1 cup milk chocolate chips
(1 6-ounce package)

Preheat oven to 350°F. Combine crust ingredients and mix at medium speed for 2-3 minutes or until particles are fine. Pat firmly into ungreased 13x9x2-inch pan. Place pecans over the unbaked crust. Prepare the caramel layer as follows: in heavy 1-quart saucepan, combine brown sugar and butter. Cook over medium heat until the entire surface of the mixture begins to boil. Boil ½-1 minute, stirring constantly. Pour evenly over the pecans and crust. Bake near center of oven for 18-22 minutes or until entire caramel layer is bubbly and crust is light golden brown. Remove from oven and immediately sprinkle with chocolate chips. Allow chips to melt slightly (2-3 minutes), then swirl as they melt. Leave some whole for a marble effect. Cool completely before cutting. Makes about 48 bars.

NOTE: Don't put these in the refrigerator before cutting or the chocolate will break. If milk chocolate morsels are unavailable you may use chopped chocolate kisses.

– Connie Cavett
Jan Foster

Microwave Coconut Chews

Crust

⅓ cup confectioners sugar
⅓ cup margarine or butter, softened
¾ cup all purpose or whole wheat flour

Filling

1 egg
½ cup packed brown sugar
1 tablespoon all purpose flour
¼ teaspoon baking powder
¼ teaspoon salt
¼ teaspoon vanilla
¼ cup walnuts
¼ cup coconut

Orange Frosting

1 tablespoon margarine or butter
1 cup confectioners sugar
1 tablespoon orange juice
1 teaspoon lemon juice

To make crust: mix confectioners sugar and margarine. Stir in flour. Press firmly and evenly in an 8x8x2-inch microwave-safe baking dish. Elevate baking dish on inverted dinner plate in microwave and microwave uncovered on medium (50%) for 2 minutes; rotate dish ¼ turn and microwave until mixture appears almost dry, 2-4 minutes.

To make filling: mix filling ingredients and spread over cooked layer. Microwave (unelevated) uncovered on medium (50%) for 3 minutes; rotate baking dish ¼ turn and microwave until filling is set, 3-5 minutes longer. Let cool on heatproof surface (do not use rack).

To make frosting: place margarine in a 2-cup glass measure. Micro-wave uncovered until melted, about 15 seconds. Add confectioners sugar, orange juice, and lemon juice; mix until smooth.

Frost cookie mixture and cut into 2-inch bars. Makes about 20 cookies.

NOTE: Make *Microwave Pecan Chews* by substituting ½ cup chopped pecans for the walnuts and coconut.

– Louise Young

Peanut Butter Chocolate Chip Bars

½ cup chunky peanut butter
⅓ cup margarine
¾ cup brown sugar
¾ cup white sugar
2 eggs
2 teaspoons vanilla
1 cup flour
1 teaspoon baking powder
¼ teaspoon salt
1½ cups semi-sweet chocolate
   chips

Cream together peanut butter, margarine, and brown and white sugars. Add eggs and vanilla and blend. Add flour, baking powder, and salt. Mix well. Stir in chocolate chips. Put in greased 13x9-inch pan. Bake at 350°F for 25 minutes. Cool and cut into bars. Makes 2-3 dozen.

– Susan Scott

Seven-Layer Cookies

Mixed and baked in one pan

½ cup butter or margarine
1½ cups graham cracker crumbs
1 cup chopped nuts
1 (6-ounce) package semi-sweet
   chocolate pieces
1 (6-ounce) package butterscotch
   pieces
1⅓ cups flaked coconut
1 (15-ounce) can sweetened
   condensed milk

Preheat oven to 350°F. To melt the butter, place it in a 13x9-inch pan and place the pan in the oven while it is preheating. (If using a glass pan, heat the oven to 325°F.) Mix graham cracker crumbs with melted butter and press mixture on bottom of pan. Sprinkle with nuts, chocolate and butterscotch pieces, and coconut. Pour sweetened condensed milk over coconut. Bake 30-35 minutes or until lightly browned. Cool and cut into bars. Makes about 36 bars.

NOTE: Cookies will cut better if they've cooled in the refrigerator first. Store in an airtight container.

– Brenda McCloud

Terri's Date Bars
Sinfully delicious

1 cup (2 sticks) butter
1 pound pitted dates
1½ cups water
1 cup sugar
2 cups white flour
2 cups wheat flour
1 cup brown sugar
2 teaspoons baking powder
⅛ teaspoon salt

Preheat the oven to 350°F. Melt the butter and let it cool. In a saucepan, mix the dates, water, and sugar and cook until the mixture gets thick; reserve. Mix together the white flour, wheat flour, brown sugar, baking powder, and salt. Add the melted butter. Press ½ of this mixture in a 9-inch square baking dish. Add the date mixture on top. Cover with the second half of the flour mixture and press lightly. Cook in the preheated 350°F oven until golden brown, approximately 30 minutes. Cut into 2-inch squares. Makes about 20 squares.

– Gigi Roberts

"Quick Serve" Lemon Bars

1 cup (2 sticks) butter
2 cups flour
½ cup confectioners sugar
Pinch salt
5 tablespoons flour
2 cups sugar
4 eggs
Juice of 2 lemons
Grated rind of 1 lemon
Confectioners sugar for dusting
   top of cookies

Mix butter, 2 cups flour, confectioners sugar, and salt with pastry blender until the mixture is crumbly. Pat evenly into a 15x10-inch jelly roll pan. Bake at 350°F for 20 minutes. While crust is baking make topping by mixing together 5 tablespoons flour and sugar. Add eggs, lemon juice and rind; mix well. Pour over partially baked crust and bake 25 minutes more. Cut into squares and dust with confectioners sugar. Makes 48 bars.

NOTE: If you love lemon, you'll love these!

– Joan Kundis

Nanaimo Bars

Named after a town in British Columbia, Canada

Crust

½ cup butter
½ cup sugar
5 tablespoons powdered cocoa
1 teaspoon vanilla extract
1 egg, lightly beaten
1½ cups graham cracker crumbs
1 cup chopped walnuts

Icing

2 cups confectioners sugar
½ cup butter, softened
3 tablespoons English dessert mix
   or egg custard mix
2 tablespoons milk
4 ounces semi-sweet chocolate

To make the crust: place the butter, sugar, cocoa, and vanilla in a saucepan. Cook, stirring, until sugar is dissolved; add egg and mix well. Remove from heat and stir in graham cracker crumbs and nuts. Pack into 12x8-inch pan and refrigerate until cooled.

To make icing: combine the confectioners sugar, butter, dessert or custard mix, and milk, beating well. Spread over the crust and refrigerate for 30 minutes. Melt chocolate in the top of a double boiler placed over simmering water and then pour the melted chocolate evenly over the icing. Refrigerate once more until chilled. To serve, cut into squares. Makes 24.

– Helen Retty

Pumpkin Layer Cookies
Try in place of pumpkin pie

1 box pound cake mix
3 eggs
2 tablespoons butter, melted
4 teaspoons pumpkin pie spice
1 (8-ounce) package cream cheese, softened
1 (15-ounce) can sweetened condensed milk
1 (16-ounce) can solid pack pumpkin
½ teaspoon salt
1 cup chopped pecans

Prepare crust by combining pound cake mix, 1 egg, butter, and 2 teaspoons of the pumpkin pie spice. Mix until crumbly. Grease the bottom of a jelly roll pan or a 13x9-inch glass dish and pat in the crust mixture. Do not bake.

Prepare filling mixture by beating cream cheese until fluffy. Add remaining 2 eggs, condensed milk, pumpkin, remaining 2 teaspoons of pumpkin pie spice and salt. Mix until thoroughly blended. Pour over crust. Sprinkle nuts on top. Bake at 350°F for 35 minutes. Cool in the refrigerator. (Cookies will be custardy when removed from the oven but will firm up when cooled.) When cool, cut into squares. Makes 36.

– Cairn Ustler

Honey Oat Bran Bars

4 cups bran flakes
½ cup chopped nuts
½ cup raisins
⅓ cup margarine
⅓ cup honey
⅓ cup firmly packed brown sugar

Lightly grease 9x9x2-inch baking pan. In a large bowl, toss together cereal, nuts, and raisins; set aside. In a 2-quart saucepan, combine margarine, honey, and brown sugar; bring mixture to a boil over medium heat, stirring constantly. Boil for 5 minutes. Pour mixture over cereal mixture and toss to coat well. Press evenly into the prepared pan; let stand 1 hour. Cut into 2x1½-inch bars. Store in a tightly covered container. Makes 24.

– Darlene Holley

Easy Toll-House Cookies

⅔ cup margarine
½ cup granulated sugar
½ cup brown sugar
1 egg
1 teaspoon vanilla
½ teaspoon soda
½ teaspoon salt
1½ cups flour
1 (6-ounce) package semi-sweet
   chocolate chips
1 cup chopped pecans, optional

Blend the margarine and sugars together. Add the egg, vanilla, soda, and salt and mix well. Gradually stir in the flour and mix well. Add chocolate chips and optional nuts. Drop by the teaspoonful on ungreased cookie sheets. Bake at 375°F for 8-10 minutes. Makes 3 dozen cookies.

NOTE: One of the best and easiest chocolate chip cookies.

Crunchy Heath Bar Cookies

1½ cups sifted flour
½ teaspoon baking soda
½ teaspoon salt
½ cup margarine
¾ cup brown sugar
1 egg
1 teaspoon vanilla
1 cup finely chopped Heath Bar
   candy (21 miniature Heath
   Bars)
⅓ cup coarsely chopped pecans,
   optional

Sift together the flour, soda, and salt. Cream the margarine, sugar, egg, and vanilla together until smooth and creamy. Stir in the flour mixture; blend in the chopped candy bars. Stir in optional pecans. Drop by tablespoons on a greased baking sheet. Bake at 350°F for 12-15 minutes. Makes 3 dozen cookies.

Pineapple Drop Cookies
Unusual

2 cups all purpose flour
1 teaspoon baking powder
½ teaspoon baking soda
½ teaspoon salt
½ cup butter
1 cup firmly packed brown sugar
1 egg
1 teaspoon vanilla
¾ cup crushed pineapple, drained
¾ cup chopped walnuts
½ cup raisins

Preheat oven to 350°F. Sift together flour, baking powder, baking soda and salt. In a large bowl, cream together butter and brown sugar. Add egg and vanilla, stirring to blend. Add pineapple. Mix well. Gradually add sifted ingredients, mixing well after each addition. Fold in walnuts and raisins. Drop cookie mixture by heaping teaspoons onto ungreased cookie sheet. Bake in preheated oven for 8-10 minutes. Makes about 48 cookies.

– Esther Treese

Crescents
Mouthwatering

2 sticks butter
5 tablespoons confectioners sugar
2 teaspoons vanilla
1 tablespoon warm water
2 cups flour
2 cups walnuts or pecans, chopped
Confectioners sugar for dusting on baked cookies

Cream butter; add sugar, vanilla, and water, and beat until thoroughly combined. Beat in flour. Stir in nuts. Shape cookie dough into crescents. Bake on greased cookie sheet at 300°F for 20 minutes or until bottoms are lightly browned. Sprinkle with confectioners sugar as soon as they are removed from the oven. Makes approximately 36 cookies.

– Esther Treese

Peanut Butter Cup Cookies

Novelty cookies

1 (20-ounce) roll refrigerated peanut butter cookie dough
1 (9-ounce) bag Reese's Peanut Butter Cups (36 pieces); (place in freezer several hours before using)

Preheat oven to 350°F. Spray 3 miniature muffin pans with no stick cooking spray. Slice the cookie dough roll into nine 1-inch slices. Cut each slice into quarters, making 36 pieces. Drop each piece into a muffin cup. Bake for 10-12 minutes. While the cookies are baking, remove the peanut butter cups from the freezer and unwrap. Remove the cookies from the oven. Push 1 peanut butter cup into the center of each cookie. Let cookies set for a few minutes and then place in the freezer for a few minutes to set the chocolate. Remove from freezer and let cool completely before removing cookies from muffin cups. Makes 36 cookies.

Kids' Favorite Sugar Cookies

Make lemonade stands instantly successful

1 cup sugar
1 cup margarine, softened
1 egg
1 teaspoon vanilla extract
2 cups plus 2 tablespoons flour
½ teaspoon cream of tartar
½ teaspoon baking soda
⅛ teaspoon salt
Sugar to roll cookies in
Nonpareils, cookie sprinkles, and/or cookie crystals for decoration (optional)

Cream sugar and margarine. Add egg and vanilla and beat until fluffy. Sift flour, cream of tartar, baking soda, and salt together; add to sugar mixture and beat well. Chill for at least 1 hour or up to 24 hours. Roll 1 teaspoon of dough into a small ball; roll ball in sugar and place on ungreased cookie sheet. Flatten each ball with the heel of your hand and sprinkle with decoration if you wish. Bake at 350°F for 8-10 minutes. Makes 6 dozen cookies.

Goof Balls

1 stick margarine or butter
1 cup sugar
1 cup chopped dates
1 egg, beaten
2 cups pecans or 1 cup pecans and
   1 cup walnuts
2 cups crisp rice cereal
1 to 1½ cups confectioners sugar

Place margarine and sugar in a large saucepan; bring to a boil and boil for 10 minutes. Add dates, beaten egg, nuts, and rice cereal. When mixture is cool, form into 1½-inch balls and roll in confectioners sugar. Makes 24 cookies.

– Susan Scott

Peanut Butter Chews

½ cup sugar
½ cup light corn syrup
1 cup smooth peanut butter
Pinch salt
½ teaspoon vanilla
2 cups crisp rice cereal

Melt sugar and corn syrup in a frying pan over low heat. Add peanut butter, salt, and vanilla and stir until melted. Add cereal and stir until well blended. Turn into an 8-inch square baking dish sprayed with no stick cooking spray. Cool and cut into squares. Makes 16 cookies.

– Susan Scott

Christmas Balls

12 ounces dried apricots, diced
1½ cups pecans
2 cups cranberries
1 tablespoon fresh gated orange
   rind
¼ cup butter
1 (16-ounce) package
   confectioners sugar
1 (13-ounce) package graham
   cracker crumbs
1 (7-ounce) package coconut
   flakes

Chop apricots, pecans and cranberries in food processor. Add orange rind, butter, sugar and graham cracker crumbs. Mix well. Chill mixture for 2 hours. Roll mixture into balls and then roll in coconut. Store chilled. They will stay fresh for 3 weeks.

– Suzanne McCutchen

Paula's Christmas Candy

Hard to believe its homemade chocolate

4 pounds high quality milk chocolate
2 to 3 pounds pecans, broken into fourths

Place 2 pounds chocolate in a large saucepan and melt over warm to low heat, stirring frequently. Stir in 1-1½ pounds pecan pieces. Drop by tablespoons on a baking sheet. Put sheet in freezer for 10 minutes to harden. Remove and store tightly covered. Repeat procedure with remaining ingredients. Makes about 6 dozen pieces of candy.

NOTE: This candy lasts for up to two months if you keep it in the refrigerator. It's a great make-ahead holiday gift.

– Paula Preston

Two Minute Microwave Fudge

1 (16-ounce) box confectioners sugar
½ cup cocoa
¼ teaspoon salt
¼ cup milk
1 tablespoon vanilla
½ cup butter
1 cup nuts

Stir sugar, cocoa, salt, milk, and vanilla until partially blended. Put butter on top of this mixture and microwave on high for 2 minutes. Stir well. Add nuts and pour into an 8x8x2-inch pan and refrigerate for at least 1 hour before serving. Makes about 32 servings.

– Cindy Sturla

PIES

Banana Split Pie

A unique spin-off of the real thing

2 cups confectioners sugar
2 sticks butter, melted and cooled
2 eggs
1 (9-inch) prepared graham
  cracker pie crust
5 bananas, sliced
1 (20-ounce) can crushed
  pineapple, drained
2 (8-ounce) containers frozen
  whipped dessert topping,
  thawed
½ cup (or to taste) crushed pecans
½ cup (or to taste) chopped
  maraschino cherries
Canned chocolate syrup to drizzle
  over the top of pie

Beat confectioners sugar, butter, and eggs together for 15 minutes. Place mixture in pie crust. Place sliced bananas on cream filling and cover with crushed pineapple. Cover the bananas and pineapple with frozen whipped dessert topping. Sprinkle crushed pecans and chopped maraschino cherries over the dessert topping. Drizzle chocolate syrup over all. Serve immediately. (May be stored briefly in refrigerator.) Makes 8 servings.

– Penny Smith

Cherry-Berry Pie

1 (10-ounce) package frozen red
  raspberries, thawed
¾ cup sugar
3 tablespoons cornstarch
¼ teaspoon salt
1 (20-ounce) can tart red cherries,
  drained
2 (9-inch) pie crusts (one for the
  bottom crust and one for
  latticework or plain top crust)

Drain raspberries, reserving syrup. Add enough water to syrup to measure 1 cup. In a large saucepan mix sugar, cornstarch, and salt. Stir in raspberry syrup and drained red cherries. Cook and stir over medium high heat until bubbly; cook and stir for 1 more minute. Remove from heat; stir in raspberries. Cool 10 minutes. Pour filling into bottom pie crust. Cover with plain or latticework top crust. Bake at 375°F for 35-40 minutes. Makes 8 servings.

– Ellen Roche

Lemon Ice Box Pie

1 cup graham cracker crumbs
3 tablespoons flour
½ cup butter, melted
3 eggs, separated
1 (15-ounce) can sweetened
   condensed milk
Juice of 2 lemons
4 to 6 tablespoons sugar

Make crust by mixing graham cracker crumbs, flour, and butter. Pack in a 9-inch pie plate. Cook at 300°F for 15 minutes. Let cool.

Make filling by beating egg yolks until lemony yellow. Add condensed milk and juice from lemons. Pour into cooled pie crust. Refrigerate until firm.

Beat egg whites with 4-6 tablespoons of sugar to make meringue. Spread over chilled pie and cook until meringue is nicely browned, about 10 minutes at 400°F. Store any leftovers in the refrigerator. Makes 8 servings.

– Anita Vining

Strawberry Pie Delicious

1 cup sugar
¼ cup cornstarch
½ teaspoon salt
4 cups fresh strawberries, sliced
½ cup crushed pineapple, drained
2 tablespoons margarine
Milk
2 (9-inch) unbaked pie crusts

Combine the sugar, cornstarch, and salt. Mix well. Add strawberries and drained crushed pineapple. Place in pie crust. Dot with 2 tablespoons margarine. Cut out strips from remaining pie crust and place over pie filling in a lattice work design. Brush with milk. Bake at 425°F for 10 minutes; then bake at 350°F for 30-40 minutes. Makes 8 servings.

– Susan Scott

Cherry Cheese Pies

Two pies for the work of one

2 (9-inch) unbaked pie shells
1 cup chopped pecans
3 cups sifted confectioners sugar
1 (8-ounce) package cream
  cheese, softened
1 (8-ounce) container frozen
  whipped dessert topping,
  thawed
1 tablespoon almond or vanilla
  extract
2 (21-ounce) cans cherry pie filling

Divide the pecans and press into the pie crusts; bake at 400°F for 8-10 minutes. Cool.

Gradually cream the sugar with the cream cheese. Add the dessert topping and almond or vanilla extract. Fill pie crusts and chill.

If you wish you may prepare the pie up to this point and freeze. When ready to use, thaw and proceed as below.

When ready to serve, top each pie with 1 can of cherry pie filling. Store in refrigerator. Makes 2 pies - 16 servings.

– Beth Macomber

Hot Fudge Pie

Definitely not health food but oh so good

2 squares unsweetened chocolate
1 stick margarine
1 cup sugar
2 eggs, slightly beaten
¼ cup flour
⅛ teaspoon salt
1 teaspoon vanilla
½ cup chopped nuts, optional
1 (8-inch) unbaked pie crust,
  optional

Melt chocolate and margarine in microwave or in top of double boiler. Remove from source of heat and immediately stir in sugar. Add eggs, flour, salt, vanilla, and optional nuts. Pour into a greased 8-inch pie pan or a pie pan with an unbaked pie crust. Bake at 350°F for 30 minutes. Let stand 10 minutes and then serve with whipped cream or ice cream. Makes 8 servings.

– Connie Cavett

Cheesy Lemon Pie

Try various toppings

1 (8-ounce) package light cream cheese or Neufchatel cheese
½ cup sugar
2 eggs
2 to 3 tablespoons lemon juice (depending on desired tartness)
1 teaspoon vanilla
1 teaspoon grated lemon peel, optional
1 (8-inch) pie shell, baked and cooled

In a small mixing bowl or food processor, combine the first 6 ingredients and blend well. Pour into the baked crust. Bake pie at 350°F for 20-25 minutes until slightly firm in the center. Cool and refrigerate at least 1 hour before serving. Makes 8 servings.

NOTE: This pie is delicious without any additions. However, it lends itself well to variations. It can be garnished with whipped cream, chocolate shavings, blueberry pie filling, or anything your imagination comes up with. You may use a graham cracker or chocolate cookie crust if you wish.

Quickie Krackle Pie

Ultimate chocolate

1 (8-ounce) Hershey's Krackle Bar (no substitutions)
1 (½-pint) carton (1 cup) whipping cream
1 (9-inch) graham cracker pie crust, cooked and cooled

Melt Krackle Bar over hot water. Whip cream until stiff. Fold warm chocolate into the whipped cream. Fill the graham cracker crust. Chill until firm - at least 4 hours or overnight. Serves 8.

Chocolate Cheese Pie

1 (8-ounce) package cream
  cheese, softened
1 (3-ounce) package cream
  cheese, softened
¾ cup sugar
¼ cup cocoa
2 eggs
1 teaspoon vanilla extract
½ cup chilled whipping cream
1 (6-ounce, 8-inch) packaged
  crumb crust
Cherry pie filling or whipped
  cream for topping

Heat oven to 350°F. In large mixer bowl, combine cream cheese and sugar; beat well. Blend in cocoa, scraping sides of bowl and beaters frequently. Add eggs and vanilla; blend well. Blend in whipping cream. Pour into crust. Bake 35-40 minutes. (Center will be soft but will set upon cooling.) Cool to room temperature. Cover and chill several hours or overnight. Garnish with pie filling or whipped cream. Makes 6-8 servings.

– Gail Loeffler

Grasshopper Pie

1 cup chocolate wafer crumbs
¼ cup sugar
5 tablespoons melted butter
¼ cup milk
1 pound mini marshmallows
½ cup green crème de menthe
¼ cup white crème de cocoa
3 drops green food coloring
4 cups whipping cream, whipped

Make chocolate wafer crust by mixing the chocolate wafer crumbs, sugar, and melted butter together. Press into a 9-inch pie plate and chill. Make pie filling by heating milk and marshmallows over low heat until marshmallows are melted. Cool. Stir in liqueurs and food coloring. Fold into whipped cream. Pile into chocolate crust and freeze until firm. Let stand for 10 minutes before cutting. Makes 8 servings.

– Esther Treese

Chocolate Marshmallow Pie

Great for the holidays

Crust
12 graham crackers, crushed
3 tablespoons butter, melted
Filling
15-20 large marshmallows
¼ cup milk
½ pint heavy whipping cream, whipped
1 square bitter chocolate
½ teaspoon vanilla
½ cup walnuts

Mix graham crackers and butter. Mix well and pat into a pie plate. Place marshmallows and milk in a double boiler and heat until marshmallows are melted (or heat in microwave until marshmallows are melted). Cool. Add whipped cream. Chip in bitter chocolate. Add vanilla and walnuts and mix all together. Pour filling into graham cracker crust. Set in the refrigerator for at least 2 hours. Pie is best if it is refrigerated overnight. Serves 8.

– Judith E. Vasterling

Chocolate Chip Pecan Pie

The ultimate for sweet lovers

1 cup sugar
½ cup flour
2 eggs, beaten
¾ cup butter, melted
1¼ cups chopped pecans
1 cup chocolate chips
1 teaspoon vanilla
1 (9-inch) pie shell, unbaked

Combine sugar and flour; add eggs. Stir in melted butter. Add pecans, chocolate chips and vanilla. Pour into pie shell. Bake for 1 hour at 325°F. *Do not refrigerate.* Serve with whipped cream. Makes 8 servings.

– Carolyn Nelson

Peanut Fudge Pie
Very sweet and very rich

4 ounces cream cheese, softened
1 cup confectioners sugar
½ cup creamy peanut butter
½ cup milk
1 (8-ounce) container frozen
  whipped dessert topping,
  thawed
1 cup hot fudge sauce, warmed
¼ cup chopped peanuts
1 (9-inch) graham cracker crust,
  baked and cooled

Whip cream cheese until fluffy. Beat in sugar and peanut butter. Slowly add milk and blend thoroughly. Fold in dessert topping. Reserve. Pour warmed fudge sauce into pie crust and spread evenly; cover with cream cheese/peanut butter mixture. Sprinkle with peanuts. Freeze until firm. Serves 8.

– Susan Scott

Easy Baked Custard Pie
Comfort food

¼ cup (½ stick) margarine, melted
1 (12-ounce) can evaporated milk
  or evaporated skim milk
2 heaping tablespoons plain or
  self-rising flour
1 cup sugar
1 teaspoon vanilla
1 (9-inch) deep-dish pie crust,
  baked and cooled

Blend margarine, evaporated milk, flour, sugar, and vanilla in a food processor for 3 minutes. Pour into the pie crust. Bake at 400°F for 10 minutes; continue to bake at 325°F for 25-35 minutes. Pie should jiggle in the center when removed from the oven. Leave on the counter to continue to cook and cool before cutting. Refrigerate when cool. Serves 8.

– Dottie Stanton

Southern Pecan Pie
Scrumptious

1 cup sugar
¾ cup corn syrup
½ cup butter, melted
⅛ teaspoon salt
1 teaspoon vanilla
3 eggs, beaten
1½ cups pecans
1 (9-inch) pie shell, uncooked

Mix sugar, syrup, butter, salt and vanilla. Add eggs and beat well. Stir in nuts. Fill pie shell. Bake for 10 minutes at 400°F. Then lower temperature to 350°F and finish cooking for 30-35 minutes. Makes 8-10 servings.

– Becky Dunn

Yankee Pecan Pie
The original Ritz Mock Apple Pie

3 egg whites
1 cup sugar
24 Ritz crackers, crushed
½ cup chopped pecans
Frozen whipped dessert topping or whipped cream
Grated chocolate to taste

Beat egg whites until very stiff, gradually adding sugar. Fold in crackers and pecans. Pile in an 8-inch pie plate that is lightly greased. Bake at 375°F for 15 minutes. When cool, cover with whipped dessert topping and grated chocolate. Refrigerate. Makes 8 servings.

NOTE: Originally known as Ritz Mock Apple Pie. Also known as Mystery Pie and No Name Pie.

– Betty Guthrie

Osgood Pie
Freezes beautifully

2 eggs, separated
½ cup (1 stick) margarine
1 cup sugar
½ cup raisins
½ cup chopped pecans
½ teaspoon cinnamon
½ teaspoon allspice
2 teaspoons cocoa
1 teaspoon vinegar
1 (9-inch) unbaked pie crust

Beat the egg yolks and add to the margarine and sugar; mix until well blended. Add the raisins, pecans, cinnamon, allspice, cocoa, and vinegar; mix well. Beat the egg whites until stiff and stir into the raisin/pecan mixture. Pour into the unbaked pie shell. Bake at 375°F for 10 minutes; reduce the heat to 325°F and bake for 30 more minutes. Serves 6-8.

NOTE: Osgood Pie originated in the South. It's name is believed to have come from the words "Oh, so good". It freezes beautifully.

Date Macaroon Pie

3 egg whites
12 Saltine crackers, crumbled
12 dates, chopped
½ cup chopped nuts
½ teaspoon baking powder
1 cup sugar
1 teaspoon almond extract
1 teaspoon water

Beat egg whites stiff. Fold in remaining ingredients. Bake in a buttered 9-inch pie plate at 350°F for 20-30 minutes. Serve with whipped or ice cream. Makes 8 servings.

DESSERTS

Amaretto Oranges

2 large navel oranges, peeled and
  sliced thinly
2 tablespoons Amaretto

Place oranges in storage container
and sprinkle with Amaretto. Cover
and refrigerate overnight. Serves 4

NOTE: If you substitute Grand Marnier for the Amaretto and sprinkle
the oranges with 2 teaspoons
chopped pistachio nuts, this is
called *Oranges Casablanca.*

Strawberries à L'Orange
Light and tasty

¾ cup strawberry preserves
½ cup orange juice
3 tablespoons Cognac
2 tablespoons wine vinegar
1 quart ripe strawberries, halved

Whisk preserves, orange juice,
cognac and vinegar. Stir in strawberries. Let macerate at room
temperature, stirring occasionally at
least 4 hours. Makes 6 servings.

Almond Cream
Summertime special

1 cup sour cream
3 tablespoons confectioners sugar
1½ tablespoons almond liqueur
1 teaspoon almond extract
4 cups assorted fresh fruit such
  as strawberries, pineapple,
  bananas, blueberries

Combine the first 4 ingredients.
Cover and chill. Serve over fresh
fruit. Serves 4-6.

Raspberry Cream
Almost replaces chocolate

1 (3-ounce) package raspberry
  gelatin
1 cup boiling water
½ pint (1 cup) vanilla ice cream
1 (12-ounce) package frozen
  raspberries

Dissolve the gelatin in the boiling
water. Add raspberries and stir until
broken up. Stir in ice cream. Chill
until set. Serves 4-6.

Chocolate Mousse
Very, very rich

1 (6-ounce) package semi-sweet or
milk chocolate chips

2 eggs

2 tablespoons rum or coffee
flavored liqueur (optional)

3 tablespoons strong hot coffee
(may be made from instant)

¾ cup milk, scalded

Optional

Semi-sweet chocolate cups (found
in gourmet section of grocery
store)

Whipped cream or frozen whipped
dessert topping, thawed

Chocolate shavings

Place chocolate chips, eggs, and liqueur in a blender. Add *hot* coffee and *hot* scalded milk and blend together on high speed for no longer than 2 minutes. (If you blend longer, the mixture won't set.) Place in individual dessert dishes, a 1-quart bowl, or individual chocolate cups. Chill well. Garnish with whipped cream or thawed whipped dessert topping and/or chocolate shavings. Serves 4.

Variation: **Chocolate Mousse Filled Angel Food Cake**

Double the mousse recipe. Hollow out the center of a 14-ounce angel food cake. Fill the center with half of the mousse and replace the cut out portion of cake. Cover the cake with the rest of the mousse and garnish with whipped cream and chocolate shavings. Serves 8.

– Carole Adler

Peppermint Bavarian

Candy cane farewell

1 envelope unflavored gelatin
2 cups milk
½ teaspoon salt
¼ pound peppermint candy, crushed (may use crushed candy canes)
1 (½ pint) carton whipping cream, whipped

Dissolve gelatin in ¼ cup of the milk. Scald the remaining milk in top of a double boiler or a heavy pan. Add salt and crushed candy to the milk and heat until the candy melts. Stir in the dissolved gelatin. Cool. When partially set, fold in the whipped cream. Pour into a 1-quart mold and refrigerate overnight. Serve with *Hot Chocolate Sauce* (see following recipe.) Serves 8.

– Bonnie Smith

Hot Chocolate Sauce

¼ cup margarine
2 squares unsweetened chocolate
1½ cups sugar
1 cup evaporated milk
Dash salt
1 teaspoon vanilla

Melt the margarine and chocolate in a saucepan or double boiler over low heat. A little at a time, stir in alternately the sugar and evaporated milk. Add the salt and vanilla. Cook for 10-15 minutes stirring occasionally. Cool somewhat before serving - it will thicken a little. Makes about 1½ cups

NOTE: This sauce is specifically for serving with *Peppermint Bavarian* but it is great for any recipe calling for a chocolate sauce. It can be made ahead; reheat on the stove or in the microwave. Store in the refrigerator.

– Bonnie Smith

Blueberry Delight

Also a delightful salad

2 (3-ounce) packages Concord
grape gelatin
2 cups boiling water
1 (16-ounce) can crushed
pineapple, undrained
1 (21-ounce) can blueberry pie
filling
Topping
1 (8-ounce) package cream cheese
1 (8-ounce) carton sour cream
⅓ cup sugar
Vanilla to taste

Dissolve gelatin in boiling water;
add undrained pineapple and
blueberry pie filling; mix well. Place
in refrigerator and set until firm
(overnight). Make topping by whipping cream cheese, sour cream,
sugar and vanilla together until
smooth. Spread over the firmly set
gelatin mixture. Serves 6-8.

– Jody Schrenk

Pink Dessert

Refreshing

1 (11-ounce) can mandarin
oranges
1 (20-ounce) can crushed
pineapple
1 (8-ounce) container frozen
whipped dessert topping,
thawed
1 (16-ounce) carton cottage cheese
1 (3-ounce) package strawberry
gelatin

Drain fruits. Mix fruit, dessert
topping, and cottage cheese together. Sprinkle gelatin over and fold
into mixture. Chill. Stir before serving. Serves 6-8.

NOTE: You can store this dessert in
the refrigerator for up to a week.

– Gunda Fletcher

Chiffon Cheesecake

1¼ cups crushed graham cracker
  crumbs
3 tablespoons sugar
⅓ cup margarine, melted
1 (3-ounce) package lemon gelatin
1 cup boiling water
3 tablespoons lemon juice
2 (8-ounce) packages cream
  cheese
1⅓ cups sugar
1½ teaspoons vanilla
1 (14-ounce) can evaporated milk,
  whipped until frothy
1 cup whipping cream, whipped
  until fluffy

Make graham cracker crust by combining crumbs, sugar and melted margarine and mixing well. Press mixture into a 9-inch springform pan and bake at 350°F for 8 minutes. Cool. Meanwhile dissolve gelatin in boiling water; cool. Add lemon juice. Cream the cream cheese, sugar, and vanilla together. Add cooled gelatin mixture to the cream cheese and blend well. Fold in the whipped evaporated milk and the whipped cream. Pour onto the graham cracker crust. Chill 24 hours. Serves 8-10.

– Susan Scott

Creamy Cheesecake

Filling

12 ounces cream cheese, softened
¾ cup sugar
2 eggs
2 teaspoons vanilla
½ teaspoon lemon juice
1 prepared 9-inch graham cracker
  pie crust

Topping

1 cup sour cream
3 tablespoons sugar
1 teaspoon vanilla

Combine filling ingredients and mix well in blender or mixer. Pour into graham cracker crust and bake for 30 minutes at 350°F. It's ready when it looks like gelatin in the middle. Make topping by combining all ingredients. Spread on cheesecake and bake 5 minutes longer. Cool. Serve cold. Makes 8 servings.

– Shirley Person

So Easy Individual Cheesecakes
Party fare

14 vanilla wafers
4 (3-ounce) packages cream
  cheese, softened
⅔ cup sugar
2 eggs
1 teaspoon vanilla extract
¾ cup sour cream
¼ cup sugar
1 (10-ounce) package frozen sliced
  strawberries, thawed and
  drained.

Line muffin pans with paper liners. Place a vanilla wafer in each cup. Set pans aside.

Beat cream cheese with electric mixer until light and fluffy; gradually add ⅔ cup sugar and mix well. Add eggs and vanilla, beating well. Spoon mixture into liners, filling ⅔ full. Bake at 350°F for 10 minutes. Cool.

Combine sour cream and ¼ cup sugar; mix. Spread over each cheesecake. Top each with a heaping teaspoon of strawberries. Freeze until firm. Remove from freezer 5 minutes before serving. Makes 14 individual cheesecakes.

– Erika Eidam

Fruit Pizza I

1 (20-ounce) package refrigerated
    sugar cookie dough
1 (8-ounce) package cream cheese
½ cup sugar
2 teaspoons vanilla
Choice of fruits: sliced
    strawberries, sliced red and
    green grapes, sliced bananas,
    sliced kiwi fruit, sliced peaches,
    drained pineapple chunks,
    drained mandarin oranges,
    blueberries
¼ cup lemon juice
2 tablespoons cornstarch
¾ cup orange juice
½ cup sugar
¾ cup water

Grease a 12-inch pizza pan. Pat out cookie dough in a circle, in the shape of a pizza, with crust turned up on edges. (Do not add extra flour when working with the dough. Work dough carefully and be patient.) Bake at 350°F for 10 minutes. Cool. Mix the cream cheese, sugar, and vanilla together; spread mixture over cooled cookie crust. Arrange any of the fruit suggestions in a circular pattern over the cream cheese. Make a glaze by mixing together the lemon juice, cornstarch, orange juice, sugar, and water and boiling for 2 minutes. Cool and then spread over the fruit making sure all of the fruit is covered. Refrigerate until the glaze is set. Serves 12-14.

– Louise Young

Fruit Pizza II

1 (16-ounce) box sugar cookie mix
1 (8-ounce) package cream cheese
½ cup sugar
½ teaspoon vanilla
1 (10-ounce) jar orange
 marmalade
Choice of fruits: sliced
 strawberries, sliced red and
 green grapes, sliced bananas,
 sliced kiwi fruit, sliced peaches,
 drained pineapple chunks,
 drained mandarin oranges,
 blueberries

Prepare cookie mix and spread on a 12-inch pizza pan. Bake at 375°F for 8-10 minutes. Cool. Mix cream cheese, sugar, and vanilla together and spread on cooled cookie crust. Spread the orange marmalade over the cream cheese mixture. Arrange a choice of fruit on top of the marmalade. Cut into wedges to serve. Serves 12-14.

– Sheryl Turner

Noodle Pudding
Easily doubled or tripled

½ pound wide egg noodles
1 cup sugar
½ teaspoon salt
3 eggs, beaten
½ pound cottage cheese
¼ pound cream cheese, softened
¼ cup (½ stick) butter or
 margarine, melted
½ pint sour cream
¼ cup raisins (optional)
¼ cup nuts, chopped (optional)
4 tablespoons cinnamon sugar
 (3 tablespoons sugar and 1
 tablespoon cinnamon
 combined)

Cook noodles according to package directions. Drain. Combine noodles and all other ingredients, except cinnamon sugar, and place in 8-inch square pan. Sprinkle with cinnamon sugar and bake at 350°F for 30 minutes. Serves 4-6.

– Carole Adler

Better Than Robert Redford Dessert

Also known as Hobo Dessert

1 cup finely chopped pecans
1 cup flour
½ cup butter, softened
1 (16-ounce) package cream
  cheese, softened
1 cup confectioners sugar
1 (8-ounce) container frozen
  whipped dessert topping,
  thawed
1 (3½-ounce) package instant
  chocolate pudding
1 (3½-ounce) package instant
  vanilla pudding
2 cups milk
1 (8-ounce) container frozen
  whipped dessert topping,
  thawed
Chocolate shavings (optional)

To make layer 1: combine pecans, flour, and butter and press into a 13x9-inch pan. Bake at 350°F for 15-20 minutes; cool. *To make layer 2:* mix cream cheese and confectioners sugar together until well combined and then fold in one container of thawed whipped dessert topping; spoon over the crust layer. *To make layer 3:* whip the chocolate pudding, vanilla pudding, and milk together until thick (about 2 minutes); pour over the cream cheese layer. *To make layer 4:* spread the second container of thawed whipped dessert topping over the pudding mixture. If you wish, sprinkle chocolate shavings over the top. Serves 12.

– Donna Swenson

Saints Reward

A fitting end!

12 to 16 ladyfingers
½ cup apricot brandy
1 gallon strawberry or vanilla ice
   cream or frozen yogurt, thawed
   slightly
1 cup strawberry jam

Line the bottom and sides of an 8-inch springform pan with the ladyfingers. Sprinkle the ladyfingers with ⅔ of the brandy. Spoon ½ of the ice cream or frozen yogurt into the pan and pack it down. Pour the remaining brandy over the ice cream, turning the dish so that it runs down the sides. Fill the pan with the remaining ice cream to within ½ inch of the top of ladyfingers. Cover the tops with the jam. Freeze the dish for 6-8 hours. Apply a small amount of warm water to the bottom and lower sides of the pan and unmold it on a serving plate. Return to the freezer until serving time. Serve the dessert cut in wedges. Serves 12.

SUPER SIMPLE SUMMARY OF LOWFAT NUTRITION

Avoid:

- meat
- butter
- cheese
- eggs
- chips
- ice cream

- sour cream
- fried food
- regular milk
- cream
- poultry skin
- tropical oils or lard

- packaged food containing tropical oils
- carob
- coconut

Eat:

- seafood
- vegetables
- fruit
- skinless poultry

- grain based entrees (pasta, rice, etc.)
- skim milk, nonfat & lowfat dairy products
- polyunsaturated & monounsaturated vegetable oils

Ration:

Chocolate, peanut butter, avocados, and nuts. None of these contains cholesterol but they are very high in fat!

Conversions from High to Lowfat:

- Meat entrees to Seafood, skinless poultry & grain based entrees
- Butter to Lowfat margarine
- Cheese to Lowfat cheese
- Ice cream to Lowfat frozen yogurt, ice milk, sherbet, sorbet, nonfat frozen desserts
- Sour cream to Nonfat yogurt (stir 2 tablespoons flour or 1 tablespoon cornstarch in before cooking with it)
- Cream to Evaporated skim milk
- Tropical oils (coconut, palm) or lard to Polyunsaturated & monounsaturated oils (canola, corn, cottonseed, soybean, safflower, olive, peanut, walnut, sesame)
- Regular (whole), 2%, 1% milk to Skim milk
- Chocolate to Cocoa in cooking, chocolate syrup
- Cream cheese to Neufchatel
- Mayonnaise to Lowfat, no cholesterol mayonnaise plus half the recipe's amount in nonfat yogurt
- Eggs to Egg substitutes or egg whites
- Ricotta to Lowfat cottage cheese

Conversion Tips For Baking:

- Eggs — If a recipe calls for 4 or more eggs, don't use egg substitutes
- Oils — To substitute a lowfat cooking oil for a solid shortening use ¾ cup oil for each cup of margarine or butter. Also, ¾ tablespoon of oil equals one tablespoon margarine or butter

TASTEFUL ENTERTAINING
No-Fault Team Parties

A party is a good excuse to get together and enjoy each others' company off the tennis courts. It's easy to think up a good reason for throwing a party. The usual holidays (Christmas, Hanukkah and Valentine's Day) will do. Or choose something whimsical like Ground Hog or Earth Day. Many parties celebrate birthdays, new babies, graduations, engagements and marriages. Teams often give a season's-end party. After a season of hard work, you deserve a treat. Maybe your team will even celebrate winning a trophy.

Sometimes people are afraid to invite guests into their homes. They fear their houses are too small or the furniture too old. On the other hand, guests don't care about grand impressions at all. They care about the company and the food, not always in that order.

Then too, people may be intimidated by the idea of coordinating a party—providing refreshments, arranging entertainment and cleaning up afterwards. Actually a party will run smoothly if you break down the arrangements into separate tasks and plan each task well in advance. Careful planning is the key to successful entertaining. You don't need to be Martha Stewart or Julia Child. You do need to have a sincere desire to please your guests. Then just proceed with a little imagination and lots of organization.

Occasion - Date - Time

Choose a date which is acceptable to you and most of your intended guests. Check your calendar. If the date you choose coincides with your city's annual art festival or the National Basketball Association championship, you can expect many no-shows. Even worse, some guests may come but spend the evening sulking or staring at your TV set. Another bad choice of dates is during school holidays; too many people will be traveling. Choose a date as far in advance as possible to give most people an opportunity to attend.

A good method of choosing a date is for the hostess to pick two or three dates convenient for her. Then she asks her teammates at a meeting to raise their hands as each date is announced if they can attend on that date. She chooses the date that is acceptable to everyone. At least this method ensures that the greatest number of people will be able to attend.

Type of Party

Teams usually like to share responsibility for the party. That's why a cooperative buffet is the type of team party most often chosen. Practically speaking, team members are more willing to hostess parties when they know the whole burden of arranging, cooking, and cleaning up doesn't fall on any single individual. Cooperative dinners are also great from the standpoint of expense. No single person has to bear the cost of entertaining the whole team. Brunches, luncheons, cocktail parties and dinner parties can all be organized as cooperative buffets.

Guest List

Making the guest list for a team party is usually cut and dried. But there are still decisions to be made. Will spouses (or "significant others") be included? Will the tennis pro, tennis coach, or club management be invited? If the party is a baby shower or engagement shower do you want to invite grandmothers, siblings, best friends, and/or former team members?

The main purpose in giving a party is for everyone to have a good time. Will Charlotte's 80-year old grandmother really enjoy herself with a group of women she doesn't know or share interests with? If husbands are included in your team party they may never have met each other or possibly only at last year's tennis party.

When people other than team members are included in a team tennis party, you have to exert extra effort to ensure a successful party. When 15-20 women and their companions gather, you'll find that you have a very diverse group. Team members have the common bond of their sport and their friendship. This doesn't mean that their husbands, mothers or friends will feel comfortable with each other or have anything in common.

When non-team members are included in your party, it is your responsibility as hostess to encourage the diverse group to feel comfortable with each other.

Greet each person at the door. Try to circulate during the beginning of the party and make sure that everyone is introduced. Name tags are a nice way to help your guests remember the names of people they see rarely.

Invitations

The dates for team tennis parties have usually been decided in team meetings so it isn't absolutely necessary to call or mail a formal invitation. It is, however, a thoughtful gesture to send or pass out reminder invitations to eliminate any confusion about date or time. If the party location is new or hard to find, be sure to include a map and phone number in your invitation.

Menu

If you are in charge of a cooperative party for your tennis team, there is a way to be sure the menu will be appropriate, well-rounded, and appetizing. Choose for the main course something like a smoked turkey, ham, or lasagna. Then make a sheet telling what the main dish will be and make a sign-up list for the groups of food that you wish to have served with places for people to sign their names and their contributions. Here is an example:

Main Dish — Lasagna

Appetizer	Salad	Vegetable	Starch	Dessert
1. _____	1. _____	1. _____	1. _____	1. _____
2. _____	2. _____	2. _____	2. _____	2. _____
3. _____	3. _____	3. _____	3. _____	3. _____

This type of list will prevent such disasters as fourteen broccoli casseroles.

If you are contributing food to a buffet party, there are several things to keep in mind. Foods should be simple to eat. It's hard to manage Rock Cornish hens while balancing a plate on one's knees. If food is to be served hot, be sure it will not spoil or overcook on a hotplate or chafing dish. Any food requiring the use of a knife should be avoided unless everyone has a seat and a table. Usually all of the food at a buffet will be on one plate so avoid runny dressings and sauces. You may serve such fare in small individual dishes or ramekins which can be set on a plate. When signing up on the food list, consider the other recipes that are on the list. If the main dish is lasagna, don't offer to bring tortellini. Dishes should compliment each other—not clash. If you are unsure about what you might contribute, ask the hostess or other teammates for suggestions.

In planning for quantities, check the number of servings a recipe calls for. An old adage goes "If they like it, it serves ten; otherwise twelve." In figuring amounts for cocktail parties you can plan about ten hors d'oeuvres (or bites) per person (four bites if dinner is to follow.)

It's always nice to use make ahead recipes for a party. Then there's no last minute fuss and most catastrophes are eliminated. Many of the recipes in this book are make ahead so take advantage of their convenience. The hostess should let those bringing food know approximately when it will be served. That way the cooks can time their dishes accordingly.

One last word about planning menus. We live in a health conscious world today and you should keep in mind that many people are trying to stick to a lowfat, low cholesterol diet. Recipes with gobs of butter, cheese and cream aren't as appreciated as they were a few years ago. People feel their arteries clogging just by reading about such rich food. Don't be afraid to have a masterful cheesecake or a wonderful souffle at your party but have healthier alternatives available too. Some ways to lower fat and cholesterol are listed in this book. Keep them in mind when cooking for guests and friends.

Table Arrangements and Seating Plans

Team parties that include spouses are usually quite large so plan a seating arrangment in advance. It's important for everyone to have places to sit and set down their plates so they'll be comfortable while eating. Inadequate seating makes people feel rushed and uncomfortable. They think about hurrying through the buffet line in order to get one of the "good" seats. If your party will have over eight guests you might consider place cards. Cards prevent confusion and the rushed feeling. You can seat compatible people together. Some people prefer unassigned seating. This is fine as long as guests know where to go when it is time to eat.

Inventory your dishware and silverware. Be sure you have enough of everything. Consider using rented equipment. This is really a convenience as glasses, plates, silver, and serving dishes come clean and stacked and you just have to put them in their places. No washing and polishing and shining. There are alternatives to formal dinner service. High quality paper goods on the market today can add color and splash to your parties at minimal expense. Be sure to buy the best so your guests won't have to contend with soggy, droopy plates and plastic utensils that snap at the first sign of stress.

It's always wise to set your tables as far in advance as possible. Instead of taking up precious time on the day of the party you can set your tables several days ahead and cover them with sheets.

Buffet Table

Buffet tables should definitely be planned ahead of time. It's best to have a detailed plan as to where every serving dish, plate and serving utensil will be placed. That way you know there will be room for everything and there will be no embarrassing tugging and jostling for position for the meat platter in front of guests—or worse, not having room for all of the dishes.

Planning the buffet table presents a challenge when you hostess a cooperative buffet. From your menu list you'll know what food each person has signed up to bring. You can guess the size and shape of the serving dish. When you know the number and relative size of the serving dishes you can plan your buffet table.

Large dinner plates should be placed at the beginning of the food line. Silverware should be at the end so guests won't have to balance plates and silverware while trying to serve food. (Silver can be tied with ribbon or pipe cleaner twistums in a napkin to be picked up as a unit.) If there is no way to avoid using two hands to serve a dish, be sure there is room on either side to set the dinner plate down. If bread is being served from the buffet table, be sure it's cut cleanly through the loaf so guests don't have to tear it apart with one hand.

When planning the buffet table, don't forget a spot for a centerpiece, candles, or flowers.

Liquid Refreshments

The hostess may provide everything or a limited selection of drinks. Your group might enjoy a special drink produced in large quantities like a punch, mulled wine or cider. Even cocktails like whiskey sours, bloody marys and daiquiris can be made ahead and refrigerated. These communal festive drinks can be tied to a seasonal or holiday theme.

There is no need to spend large sums on drinks. Most guests are happy to bring their own favorites. The hostess could provide mixers. The key is to tell guests what to expect. If you do have a BYOB affair, remember to designate an accessible place to house all the guests' bottles.

Do provide coffee for dinner parties. Many people get drowsy after cocktails and hearty food. Guests are much more amusing when they are awake and alert.

Music

You don't have to have music at all but it's a great mood enhancer. If you plan to provide it, appoint somebody to change records, tapes, etc. Test your music ahead of time. Play cheerful, energetic music before food is served. It breaks the silence when the first guests arrive, which is particularly useful if they don't know each other well. Don't let the volume get so loud that people need to shout to make themselves heard over it.

Serve up quiet, tranquil music during dinner, such as ballads, classical and New Age. Don't assume all classical music is peaceful. Resume upbeat music after dinner to prevent falling asleep. If the music is danceable enough, your guests may find it irresistable.

Decorating

There are some clever inexpensive things you can do to give your home a festive feeling. Candles and flowers are the basic units of party decoration. They always give an elegant, special feeling. You can also use brightly colored balloons, bows on doors and mailboxes, holiday banners, windsocks, and Japanese lanterns or luminaria to decorate the outside of your house. It's even possible to have photographs of famous tennis players (or your teammates) blown up to poster size to line the entrance hall.

Sometimes a single item will give you an entire theme to decorate around. Perhaps you've seen colorful bandannas that you love in a discount store. Use them as place mats for a casual party and let your guests take them home as a party favor. You can devise many beautiful tables by taking your decorating cues from the season.

With a little creativity you can make clever decorations using a tennis theme. Consider using sun visors as a base for a centerpiece. Ball cans make marvelous vases; ball hoppers can hold plants. Ask the artist on your team to draw cute designs on place cards. Racquets and drink containers can be put into use. A roll of handle wrap might be used for napkin holders. This is the time to let your imagination run wild.

Games and Awards

Games can be a lot of fun at a team tennis party if you choose ones that aren't too silly or childish. Plan the games well in advance of the party so that all the props, written instructions, rules, etc. will be properly arranged.

One game that's a lot of fun to play is "Personality Quiz." Find one fact about each person who will attend the party. It should be a fact not generally known about the person such as "used to be a church organist", "lived in Nome, Alaska for six months", "has raced cars for a living", "has a degree in art history." Compose a list of these little known facts. Make enough copies of the list for each guest to have one. Now ask people to match up names of guests with each fact. The object, of course, is to get as many as possible correct. It's amazing to see the new things you'll learn about people you thought you knew pretty well. This game also helps team members learn non-tennis information about each other. It raises awareness of talent outside tennis.

Connie Cavett, team tennis hostess, introduced us to another game called "Personality Bingo." It was a big hit. Make a bingo-type grid using up to twelve boxes on an 8½x11-inch sheet of paper. In each box you list a descriptor that *could* apply to a person. You can choose descriptors from the following list or you can make up your own.

- Has won a golf trophy
- Is called by his/her middle name
- Has never filled own gas tank
- Has an unusual pet
- Was born outside of the USA
- Can turn a cartwheel
- Has the autograph of a president
- Sings in a choir
- Can speak more than one language
- Can play three instruments
- Can recite the Gettysburg Address
- Can name all the states and capitals
- Has never lived outside of Florida
- Has had something published
- Has ever owned an Edsel

- Is a twin
- Is a Viet Nam vet
- Snores
- Scuba dives
- Is a licensed pilot
- Has four or more siblings
- Has hazel eyes
- Has taken tap dance
- Has sung professionally
- Can crochet
- Was a high school quarterback
- Can name the Lennon Sisters
- Can name the members of U-2
- Has held an elected government office

The object is to talk to people at the party and find out if any of the information applies to them. When you do, you mark the name of the person who fits the description in the box. The first to complete a row vertically or horizontally wins the game. This is a particularly good game for large groups who don't know each other well because the questions serve as conversation openers. People love to find things in common and this is a good gambit to discover mutual interests.

A variation of "Personality Bingo" which is also fun is to request that each invitee submit ahead of time (or bring to the party hidden in a paper bag) an object or item that is distinctly theirs. A bird watcher might bring binoculars, a hunter might bring a mounted trophy (of the small variety), a seamstress a thimble, a reader a pair of glasses, a pilot his wings. At one party a woman who grew up in New Zealand submitted kiwi fruit. The items are placed on a table with no identification. Guests are given a list of people who submitted objects and are asked to match them by writing the name of the object next to the name of the person. Whoever gets the most correct wins.

A game that is fun at tennis parties is to make a montage by cutting out pictures of famous tennis players at various stages in their careers and pasting them on a piece of cardboard. Guests are asked to name the players to see who can name the most. (Now you know why you've been saving all those old tennis magazines.)

It's also fun to have a tennis trivia quiz. Divide participants into two groups and give each group the same list of tennis trivia questions. See which team answers the most questions correctly.

The joy of the games mentioned here is that not everyone has to participate to make them fun. Those who don't want to play don't have to feel like wet blankets. Once you get several people interested, however, the others will usually become curious and then want to join. They too will get caught up in the fun and discussion that inevitably surrounds the games.

Probably the most entertaining activity at a tennis party is a season's-end awards presentation. For many teams this is an event anticipated throughout the season. One or two people should be appointed as coordinators for the awards. The awards should be amusing. Examples are a surgical mask for the team member who serves with her mouth open; a megaphone for the soft-spoken captain who has trouble being heard; a football helmet for the unfortunate player who was hit in the head when her partner was serving a ball; a Superwoman cape for the strongest player on the team; a set of worry beads for the team's worrywart. Use your imagination and sense of humor. Ask team members for suggestions, too. The response is so great that it makes the effort worthwhile.

Party Time

When the day of the party arrives, it's time to enjoy the fruits of your planning. The most important thing to remember is to get yourself put together as well as your party. Don't greet guests at the door and then run off to the bathroom to finish your makeup. This will make guests feel ill at ease. All the food and preparation of tables should be done. Your home should be reasonably neat and clean. A messy house tells guests they aren't important enough to clean up for. Children and toys should be out of sight.

One last caution; don't rush your guests. Don't begin clearing things away too quickly yourself or let other guests do it either. Premature cleanup makes your guests think you regard them as messy nuisances and want them to leave. Then too, the sight of the hostess slaving away in the kitchen detracts from guests' enjoyment. Some of them may actually feel guilty for having fun as they wonder whether they should be doing dishes instead.

Now you know how to provide the conditions for a good party. Your guests will be grateful to you for organizing the event. They are looking forward to your party and so will you.

Cuisine Index

Team Tennis Counsel

Counsel Table of Contents

INTRODUCTION

The best way to use this handbook is to read straight through it. Afterwards return to the topics you need help with by using the Index and/or Table of Contents. The specific suggestions make more sense when you know the reasoning behind them. The partnership arrangement instructions for example, are easy to understand after you learn how important ladders are. The same topic may be found in several different sections of *Counsel* treated in different ways. Severe behavior problems, for instance, are mentioned in the chapters on teammates, partners, captains and yourself.

We have included a Bibliography. It contains great sources for additional information you may want to order as well as inspiration and psychological motivation.

PART ONE:
Team Tennis

Part One tells you how to start your team tennis experience productively. It will help non-team members decide whether to join a team and how to join a team. We explain how to set up new teams and reorganize established ones.

New team players can use Part One as instruction manuals for team construction. Established team members may find that their teams are already organized just as we suggest in Part One. Some points, however, will surely differ. Compare our recommendations with what you already have. Just a few of our ideas may propel your team from average to super.

CHAPTER 1:
Team Membership

Do you want to join a tennis team? Before you write your first league check investigate the advantages and disadvantages.

To Join (Advantages of Team Membership):

1. Ten to twenty players will be available to play with you. They are your teammates.
2. You'll spend less time on the telephone arranging matches. Just ask, "Who wants to play tomorrow?" when your teammates are gathered in one spot.
3. Team social life will add fun to your tennis.
4. If competition is new to you, your teammates will give you support while you're learning.

5. You will improve faster than if you only play social tennis. Competition makes a match mean more so you try your best.
6. You will improve faster because you'll want to help your teammates as well as yourself.
7. You will improve faster because you will often play people of higher skill levels. This forces you to try new shots and strategies. You learn to handle speed and strength.

Or Not To Join (Disadvantages of Team Membership):

1. You spend more time on tennis because of travel to matches, clinics, practices, team meetings and socializing.
2. The team's goals may not be the same as yours. Since team welfare comes first, you'll need to compromise.
3. You may find it hard to quit because of group pressure not to let the team down.

Self-assessment:

First answer these questions honestly:

1. What level of tennis skill do you want to reach?
2. Do you want to focus exclusively on tennis skills, or do you want to socialize as well?
3. Do you have the self-discipline to create a solo structured program for the advancement of your skills or do you need outside group pressure?
4. Can you get along easily in a group or are you unwilling to make the compromises groups require?
5. Do you like people as much as you like tennis?

Decision Time:

If you want to become the very best player you can be in this lifetime...

If you do not want to waste a minute on socializing or meetings...

If you can set up and maintain a training and competition schedule for yourself...

If you do not want to compromise on the amount of playing time, lineup positions or partners...

then please forget team tennis!

On the other hand,

If you want to become the very best player you can while maintaining a social life...

If you are willing to spend time helping to run your team in exchange for their schedule of matches, practices and clinics...

If you prefer to learn new activities in the company of other people...

If you will compromise on the amount of playing time, lineup position and partners...

then sign up for team tennis! We would love to have you.

CHAPTER 2:
Joining A Team

Welcome! You decided to join a team. Now let's find the best one for you. First you need a team which is appropriate for your tennis skill level. A local tennis pro can give you the name of your local U.S.T.A. affiliate. That office can tell you about your local team tennis scene and who to call. Narrow down the possibilities by cost and location. Try to pick the best one of those.

How To Know A Good Team When You See One:
1. Team members enjoy spending time together.
2. All members know that they contribute something to the team other than presenting their bodies at matches.
3. The majority rules but the minority wishes are respected.
4. The leadership is flexible; traditions can be changed or scrapped.
5. When they lose matches, the members are still friends and the whole structure does not fall apart.
6. The captain does not need inpatient psychiatric care for exhaustion at the end of the season.

Teams have individual characters and the variety is amazing. Some teams are all business --, "We're here to play tennis and that's it." Others are almost all fun --, "We're in the bottom of our league for the 8th year but we have the best parties in town and we don't care." Most teams fall somewhere in between. You could be very unhappy in an atmosphere which does not suit you. Do try to find out what kind of group it really is before you commit yourself.

Be sure you know what your needs are in terms of friendship, competition, structure, economy, etc. For example, if you want to make new friends, will you be happy on a team whose members have nothing in common with you? If your time is strictly limited, how can you cope with pressure from a team with numerous practices, round robins, clinics and social activities in addition to the matches? If your budget is tight, will you be embarrassed by inability to keep up with a jet set team in designer clothes and vehicles?

Before you sign on the dotted line with a team, read the chapter called *News For New Players* in Part Five: *Ad-On.*

Reorganizing A Bad Team:
What if you cannot find a good team? Join a bad one and wait patiently for the chance to reorganize it.

If you want to reorganize an existing team,
1. Read all the material in this book.
2. Analyze what is wrong with the team at present.
3. Design a plan to fix it.
4. Enlist support for your plan (convince your teammates).
5. Get yourself elected captain and try to implement your plan.

Creating Your Own Team

Another alternative is to start up a brand new team. To do this, read the remainder of this book and go to it.

CHAPTER 3:
How To Organize A Tennis Team

Why Bother?

Never underestimate the importance of good organization. Most team failure we have heard of resulted from chaotic structure or dictatorial management. This section will help you avoid either of them.

This information isn't just for captains. The better informed you are as a team member, the better you'll force your captain to be. Your team will improve. Someday you, too, may want to be a captain.

Basic Ingredients

The basic ingredients for a team are a home base, and a minimum number of players. Both of these must fit the rules of the tennis league that your team will be part of. Ask your tennis pro for the name of your local U.S.T.A. affiliate. This office will give you one or more league contacts to talk to. Ask for the league's rules.

Courts — How many courts does your league require? Find a home base with enough courts. Read the chapter on relationships with clubs and facilities before committing yourself to set up a team at a specific facility.

Players — Recruit a group of women interested in forming a team. You can recruit players by asking your tennis pro for names, calling your friends, posting signs at tennis facilities and notices in their newsletters and asking the league for names plus suggestions. When you have a home base and the minimum number of players needed, call a short meeting to elect officers.

Who's In Charge Here?

Teams work best as participatory democracies. In this system the majority decides upon the rules. The minority has respect and assurance that its ideas will be heard. All members participate in running the team. To run efficiently teams need rules which cover as many situations as possible and are clearly understood by all members. The easiest way to avoid personality conflicts is to enact rules before any person has a chance to antagonize anyone else by breaking an unwritten rule. Before making rules, your team needs to elect officers as follows:

- **Captain** — to organize and delegate duties for the team.
- **Co-Captain or Assistant Captain** — to assist the Captain, manage in the absence of the Captain, learn the Captain's duties in order to take over when the Captain retires.
- **Treasurer** — to handle money for dues, clinics, parties, uniforms, balls and gifts.
- **Assistant Treasurer** — to handle the Treasurer's duties in her absence.
- **Social Chairman** — to handle refreshments for home matches if customary in your league, and to handle arrangements for parties.
- **Assistant Social Chairman** — to handle the Social Chairman's duties when she is not available.

Hold a quick election of these officers. Once elected, the new officers should meet separately to draw up proposed rules for the team.

Rules And Procedures — How To Make Them And What To Do With Them

Anticipate the areas of conflict and confusion teams encounter. Set up rules in advance to minimize chaos. A clear team structure helps all the members because it lets them know where they stand. It saves time lost in bickering or guessing what they should do.

Things to make rules about are:

Clinics — It is vital to decide whether they are mandatory or voluntary. If they are mandatory, will that rule still apply to the player who doesn't play in the official match that week? Will there be any exceptions to the rule? Determine what day and time they will be held, what price will be charged, where they will be held and who the instructor will be.

Practice Sessions — Determine whether they will be mandatory or voluntary as well as the time, date, place and program.

Official Matches — One of the most important decisions your team will make is to decide who will make the lineups (assignment of players and positions for the given day's matches). Will it be the coach, captain, a combination or someone else? After this matter is decided, address the details like transportation (provide maps), bringing an extra player to avoid default, etc. Your league will provide guidelines for official matches regarding starting times, warmup, lineup changes, weather, etc.

Emergencies — The word emergency is often used to exempt people from rules. Be sure to agree on what constitutes an emergency. Some people believe a head cold constitutes an emergency while others will insist on playing after a death in the family. You may be amazed at the different interpretations and bad feelings this word can arouse.

Absences — How many are allowed from practices, matches and clinics and for what reasons?

Meetings — Are they mandatory or not? How often, when, where and why are they held?

Player Rights and Responsibilities — Will everyone on the team have the same rights (such as playing time) or will some (like substitutes) have fewer rights and responsibilities?

Weather Conditions — How windy, cold, hot, wet or snowy does it have to be before you cancel matches, clinics or practices? Your league may have rules regarding these questions for match play.

Complaints — If a player is unhappy about something, what should she do about it?

Terms of Office — How long should people stay in their elected positions? The longer anyone stays, the more efficient she should become but other people deserve the chance to learn from taking an office too. Remember that people who have little investment in the team will also have little commitment to it.

Prepare yourself for the first full team meeting by reading the chapter on team meetings. During the meeting the captain should read the proposed rules to the entire team. She should ask for suggestions and clarification. Discuss and vote on them. Type and date the approved rules and give every member a copy. Refer to them when questions come up. If you need to change a rule later, vote on the change and incorporate that change in the typed list of rules for the next season.

Committees

From time to time you will need to call for committees. Ask for volunteers to take care of these areas:

Uniforms — to research, present choices and order or buy them. See the chapter on uniforms in the Ad-On Section for detailed information about team uniforms.

Nomination of Officers — to nominate officers for the next season. This committee usually forms at the end of a tennis season.

Miscellaneous — to research and study any problem that is not solved quickly in a general discussion of the whole team. For example you might call a committee to search for a new tennis coach or to decide on off season activities.

If you have followed along so far, your team now has courts to play on, league rules to follow, officers and basic team rules. Most of these matters were set up during meetings. How did the meetings go anyway? The next chapter covers meetings in detail. It will help you pinpoint any problem areas you may have had and promote successful gatherings in the future.

CHAPTER 4:
Meetings

"Is this absolutely necessary?" That's the first question we hear when a meeting is proposed.

Yes, having good meetings is essential to building a good team. We need meetings to hear all points of view, solve and prevent problems, inform the membership, avoid numerous phone calls, elect officers and make or change team rules and policies.

We have all sat through endless, boring meetings and chaotic, useless meetings. No wonder so many teams try to avoid having meetings at all. You can eliminate meetings or reduce them to a three minute recitation of the weekly lineup. Unfortunately that system keeps people from voicing their opinions, questions and concerns. Eventually their misunderstandings and resentments grow. The longer problems go unresolved, the larger they become. The sooner problems are faced in a meeting, the better.

No, the telephone is not the answer. Here's why. Say three people hate the clinic and each calls once to discuss this with the captain for five minutes each. The captain changes the clinic parts they did not like. Two weeks later two other players call to express objections to the changes for five minutes each. Now the captain has spent 25 minutes on the telephone and some more time changing the clinic format but the problem still is not solved. All this could be avoided by a ten minute team discussion during a meeting.

There are other drawbacks to substituting telephone calls for meetings. The team members who didn't make calls begin to suspect plotting behind their backs. They resent actions taken without their knowledge or consent. At public meetings we all share our opinions. We make mutually acceptable compromises. Sometimes we even produce an original and elegant solution which delights everyone.

Weekly meetings will probably be quite brief, just covering the week's lineup and details. From time to time, however, it will be necessary to discuss other issues at length.

Running a meeting well is very important. It is better if the captain can run the meeting, but it is not essential for her to do it. If you are a captain and you think you cannot do a good job of it, pick someone to do this for you. Explain to the membership that you are not evading responsibility but making sure that your teammates will have good meetings. Most people can learn to run a good meeting by observing the following guidelines. If you are an exception, don't sacrifice team welfare out of a misbegotten sense of duty.

For good meetings we need both order and open communication. Without order a meeting deteriorates into confusion. People leave wondering why they came or frustrated at failure to accomplish anything. Open communication is equally essential because people who are not allowed to speak will nurse resentment. Later they will disrupt whatever solutions the leader believes were found at the meeting.

Creating Order

Here are some ways to create an orderly atmosphere:

Schedule the meeting. In advance of the planned meetings, tell all members:

When it will be held — Pick a time convenient for the majority.

Where it will be held — For long (more than 10 minutes) meetings, choose a comfortable place with seats, minimal distraction from sun, insects, noise and non-member interruption.

How long it will be — Make it as short as possible.

Stick to the arrangements you have made to avoid confusion and loss of confidence by the members.

Use an agenda. That is a list of items to be discussed at the meeting. Read the agenda out loud at the beginning so nobody thinks her topic will be ignored. e.g. "This is what we're going to cover today." Give members an opportunity to add to the agenda.

Make some general rules for meetings. Insist that one person talk at a time to avoid repetition leading to long meetings. e.g. "I ask you to speak in turn because I want to finish this meeting as soon as possible and I don't want to miss anything." Stick to the topic at hand. When you hear talk wandering off from the one subject you began, bring it back with such remarks as, "Let's get back to the clinic schedule." or "Let's take care of the clinic schedule first and then we can discuss the court conditions." "I think we're wandering off the topic of clinic schedules; let's get it out of the way and then we can discuss the club management."

Give out written material after the meeting to prevent people from reading and shuffling papers during discussion.

At the end of your meeting summarize your conclusions on all the agenda items. If it has been a long, complicated meeting, you may need to type up a summary and give everyone copies.

Encouraging Communication

These are the requirements and components of good, open communication:

Trouble Shooting — The meeting is the place to bring out discontent. If you have heard rumors of unhappiness, add the theme of the unhappiness to the agenda and bring it up. This can be done without revealing sources of information or putting anyone on the spot. Say, "I have heard that some players are not happy with their lineup spots. Please tell me if this is true so we can discuss it." or "I'm getting a vague feeling that some of us really aren't enjoying these practice sessions anymore. Am I right or just imagining things?" If you encourage open discussion, behind the scenes grumbling will diminish. If you know the main source of unhappiness, be sure she airs her position openly. You may have to ask her directly what she thinks after introducing the topic.

Participation — Some people talk much more than others but we all have the same number of thoughts and feelings. Encourage input from quiet people. Ask for their opinions by name if you see they haven't said anything. Look at facial expressions. If somebody is frowning, ask, "What do you really think of this idea?" or, "You don't think this is such a great plan, do you?"

Minority Opinions — People who feel they are listened to and respected are more likely to make positive contributions. Encourage opinions different from your own with such phrases as, "That's an original point of view." or, "You may very well be right and if our solution bombs, I'll be the first to admit it to you." or, "It is a good idea but right now nobody wants to go along with it. Maybe we can try it later after we give this idea a couple of months."

Group Wisdom — Encourage others to share their expertise. In this way we can use the best knowledge of team members for everybody's benefit. e.g. "Well, Mary can best explain the dues system" or, "Gloria, please explain the rules on service lets." After problematic matches, it's a good idea to ask the participants to tell everyone what the problems were on their court and how they handled them.

Common Problems At Meetings And Some Solutions For Them

Lateness — State starting times and stick to them. If you accomodate late people by a few minutes, the delay tends to get longer and longer. If we are on time, but the meeting doesn't start on time, our minds seem to conclude that the stated time is not the true time so we add on a few minutes for ourselves to get there next time. Eventually even the most punctual people will openly state, "Well it's supposed to start at 9 but they never start on time so let's go buy drinks (go to ladies room, etc.)." Make sure to tell everyone in advance that you will start on time and ask them to come in quietly if they are late.

Some teams have a system of fines per minute late. Most teams hold their weekly meetings right after clinics or practices to make sure that everyone is already on the spot.

Briefing Latecomers — You need a system to inform latecomers and absent members about what went on in the meeting. Here are some possible solutions: Have someone take notes to share later. Have the latecomers' partners inform them later. Make latecomers responsible for seeking out the information. If people are late and then start asking questions about matters already covered before they got there, say, "We covered that earlier. Please ask your partner later."

Total Turmoil — This phrase describes the situation where everybody talks at once. The solution depends partially on the personality of the leader. If you have a loud voice and a commanding presence, use it to say, "Be quiet." or any variation you prefer. If you don't, sit back and relax until everyone notices that chaos reigns and turns to you for guidance. When you can be heard, point out how this chaos extends the length of meetings. Express your own emotional reaction to the situation, e.g. "I feel so frustrated when everyone talks at once because I can only hear a few of the ideas and I know I'm missing a lot." If it's a continuous problem, ask the members for help in solving it. Admit you don't know what to do and seek suggestions. This is their team, their meeting and their responsibility too. Do not accept a role of disciplinarian quieting unruly children. Team members are equal adults.

"Stupid" Questions — First determine why a question is "stupid." Often we give this label to questions which refer to a matter thoroughly covered previously. These questions stem from not listening. Say, "We discussed that earlier; please ask somebody later." The question may stem from general inexperience with tennis. If it's easy to answer, patiently answer as briefly as possible or ask somebody else to answer it. If it's complicated, say you will explain this after the meeting and do so. Always answer as politely as possible, so you won't intimidate anyone.

Quicksand Issues — Sometimes a subject is a lot more complicated than you had realized and discussion is going nowhere. Ask three to five people to form a committee to study it, come up with all the possible solutions to bring up at the next meeting. Make sure the committee includes the people most emotionally involved in the issue.

Dueling Egos — Two individuals have very strong, emotional differences on an issue. Talk to both parties separately before a general meeting. Look for the real emotional issue underneath the surface. Does one really want more attention or less pressure? Try to come up with a creative answer for their real needs and a way for both to come out feeling as if they have saved face. Even if reconciliation is impossible, both parties must abide by majority rule.

Monopolizers — People who monopolize a meeting with their excessive verbiage are very disruptive. Try diversionary comments like, "Very good point; we need to hear some other points of view now." Or cut into a pause in a long speech with, "Good Agatha, now Ermintrude what do you think?" turning to another member. This may need to be repeated later. You can try asking her to summarize, as in, "Could you put that into just one sentence?" She may not be able to do it. If the monopolizer interrupts others, say, "Just a moment, Agatha; Ermintrude hasn't finished yet." Repeat as needed. Also try to get the gist of these monopolizers' ideas away from meeting times. Then you can present them in a brief form while giving their source full credit and glory. e.g. "Agatha has had a great idea. She thinks . . . about that subject." Take a cue from the talk show hosts on handling verbal ramblers. Oprah Winfrey says, "So you say what?" Larry King says, "What is your question?"

Side Shows — These are mini-conversations between two or three people in the middle of the general meeting. They whisper to each other while ignoring the main speaker. Just as your elementary school teacher used to do, say, "Tabitha and Nanette I couldn't hear you. Would you please tell us all what you're talking about?" Do not use a sarcastic tone. This will probably need to be repeated.

All this may seem like a lot to remember. When you see how much your meetings improve, you'll retain this material easily. A good meeting leaves everyone with a sense of accomplishment.

PART TWO:
How To Run A Tennis Team

How do individual tennis players become an organized group dedicated to victory against another group? There are four main stages in the process:

1. Deciding on the team's main goals which determine lineup policy.
2. Making a ladder.
3. Arranging partnerships (for doubles teams).
4. Composing lineups.

We will look at these in order.

CAUTION! Please be careful not to misuse the terms ladder and lineup. A ladder is a ranked list of players according to their skill. A lineup is a program naming the players for a specific day's match.

CHAPTER 5:
What Is Our Real Goal?

Defining a team's main goal may seem easy. Of course, we say, the goal must be to win the most matches. Look at it more closely though. Is that really what every member of your team wants? You may find some members who believe it is more important to play often. Others really just want to have fun. The time to clarify this is now. If you don't unearth your team's true goals, then lineups will be built on a false basis. Terrible and unnecessary misunderstandings will occur.

If your team's lineups are arranged with the idea that you will do whatever it takes to win the most matches, but most of your team members prefer

209

to just have fun, the team will break apart. That's why it is vital for every member to be absolutely honest about her team goals. Ask your team members if they want the team to win as many points as possible even though that means some individuals won't play or if they want everyone to play regularly knowing that they won't win as many points.

Next let's look at the three methods for designing lineups so you can match the policy to the team goal. The three possibilities are *strength, rotation or compromise.*

Playing To Win *(The Strength Policy)* — The team's most skilled players always play unless they are absent. These are the top players on the ladder. Less skilled players only play in case of absence of a top player.

Advantages: The team wins the most points this way. The top players improve their skills faster because they play more matches. It is easy to arrange lineups.

Disadvantages: The less skilled players may become resentful and/or lose interest. They don't improve as fast because they play fewer matches. The team splits into players and non-players.

Summary: Obviously this is the policy to choose if your team's goal is to win at any cost.

Equal Time *(The Rotation Policy)* — All players take turns playing equally often.

Advantages: Everybody has the same amount of play time so weaker players aren't resentful of stronger players. Everyone has the same opportunity to improve since they play the same amount. It is easy to arrange lineups.

Summary: This is the policy to choose if your team's goal is for each player to play the same amount no matter what her skills are like.

Something For Everyone *(The Compromise Policy)* — The stronger players play more often than the weaker players but everyone gets to play eventually.

Advantages: The team wins more points than by pure rotation though fewer than by strength. All players can increase their skills at comparable rates. It promotes good team morale.

Disadvantages: When the team loses matches, the lineup will be criticized. It is more complicated to arrange the lineups.

Summary: This is the policy to use if your team has mixed goals.

How To Decide Your Team's Goals And Lineup Policy

The members of an established team should meet at the end of a season to plan for the next season. Include all those who have signed a commitment to play for the next season. New teams must discuss this matter at their first full team meeting. Ask each person what her goals for the team are. Explain the advantages and disadvantages of all three lineup policies. Vote on the team goals to see which ones predominate. If an overwhelming majority favors one goal, choose the appropriate strength or rotation policy to fit with it. If the vote divides among two or more goals, choose a compromise lineup policy. This decision must be made by vote because it is one of the most important decisions a team makes. Under no circumstances should a coach, captain or other minority make this decision alone. If they do, the team will not enjoy the season, even if they win first prize, because of internal dissension.

Announce the decision to the team. Tell any new or prospective member what the policy for lineups will be. e.g. "Our team uses a rotation system, which means everybody gets to play the same amount. That's because most of our members think it's more important to play often than to win the most games." This clear kind of explanation prevents enlistment of people with false expectations who may create trouble if their illusions are shattered later. It is a good idea to print policy on your team rule sheet as a reminder.

The policy can be changed at any time if the majority of the team votes to change it. If you see dissatisfaction threatening to collapse your team with a pure strength system, you can move to a rotation. Or if you find yourself in close contention for a trophy and your team votes for it, you can change to a pure strength arrangement long enough to bring home trophies for everyone.

So there is no single right answer to the question, "Should we play strength or rotation?" It is a team decision. As long as it meets the team's goals, then it's the right decision.

Chapter 6:
Building A Ladder

A team must have its players ranked by skill in order to arrange lineups for match play. This ranking by skill is called a ladder. Once again, a ladder is not the same thing as a lineup. Many players do not know that their team has a ladder. Some believe that the weekly lineup *is* their team's ranking of the players by skill. Since the lineup usually changes according to absence, rotation, etc. it obviously is not the same thing. It is, however, quite possible to have a team ladder which has never been written down. Such an invisible ladder exists only in the head of the person who makes the lineups for the team. If she does not write it down, she will have great flexibility in moving players up or down. On the other hand, when it is not written down, many players will grossly over or underestimate their skills and then complain when the weekly lineup does not match their personal assessments of where their skills entitle them to play. Where there is a written ladder, a captain or coach has something to refer to in explaining lineups if controversy arises. Written ladders may also prevent misunderstandings. If you do not know your team's comparative strength, there are several ways to determine it:

Singles Challenge Ladders — Ask your tennis pro to organize a singles ladder competition. During a stated period of time players will challenge others above and below them on a list. The end result is a list with the most skilled players at the top and least skilled at the bottom. It is best for a non-team member to manage this competition because bad feelings may develop during challenges and team members may blame the unpleasantness on the unfortunate team member who organized it. The U.S.T.A. prints a valuable sheet explaining how to set up challenge ladders. See Bibliography entry #14.

Doubles Challenge Ladders — Have the tennis pro organize a doubles challenge ladder if you have already put all partnerships together. Normally this would not be the case because the ladder ranking will help you figure out how to match partners.

N.T.R.P. (National Tennis Ratings Program) — The U.S.T.A. has developed a system for tennis pros to rate the skills of players and give them ratings. Have all team members get their official ratings and then rank them in order of those numbers. The way to find out how to have players rated is by consulting your local affiliate of the U.S.T.A. Ask your tennis pro for a telephone number. An explanation of the ratings system may be obtained by mail from the U.S.T.A. See Bibliography entry #15.

Records Ladder — Make a position ladder based on previous records. Find out what position each player won in most and give her that number. Cordelia, for example, won most often in third position last season. Give her number 3. When you finish, the team may have several people with the same numbers because their records are similar in identical positions. You may assume their skill levels are close. Convert this list of names with position numbers (A) into a ladder (B) as shown in this example:

Records List A

1. Arabella
2. Beatrice
3. Cordelia, Dorcas
4. Ermintrude, Grace, Hortense, Isolde
5. Jessamine, Cleo, Myrtle, Nanette
- Gertrude (no prior record)

Ladder B

1. Arabella
2. Beatrice
3. Cordelia
4. Dorcas
5. Ermintrude
6. Grace
7. Hortense
8. Isolde
9. Jessamine
10. Cleo
11. Myrtle
12. Nanette
13. Gertrude

The way to rank different players in the same position number such as Cordelia and Dorcas is to compare their win/loss percentages. For example Cordelia won 9 of 10 matches in third position. Her percentage is 90%. Dorcas, on the other hand won 7 of 10 matches in third position. Her percentage is 70% so she will be placed below Cordelia on the ladder.

Round-Robins — Have all players play against each other, singles or doubles, and rank them according to matches won. You can vary this by only having players of comparable skill level play each other if you have records to verify those levels.

Summary — Ladders based on proven competitive performance, in other words, records, are the most valid. The second greatest controversy in team tennis after lineup policy concerns ranking players' skills. How do you know who is the best player on your team? The answer is the player who wins the most games. All other considerations are secondary. That's why a records ladder is the most accurate one for predicting future wins. What about challenge ladders? Well, singles players may not be the best doubles players and if your league plays only or predominantly doubles matches, a singles ladder may not be very helpful. Competitive matches between teammates for ladder positions, whether in singles or doubles challenges, bring out hostility between teammates. N.T.R.P. ratings do not give a valid picture of performance in actual matches. Round-robins take lots of time and also introduce the same hostility between teammates. People play differently against teammates than against outside opponents. For all these reasons we believe that ladders based on actual records, if available, are better predictors of future play.

As the season progresses you will need to change the ladder because of improved skills, injury, match results and new members. In case a player's skills improve dramatically, the match records will show it and her position should be shifted upwards. Challenge matches are not advisable because they pit team members against each other instead of welding them together against opposition teams. A new team member should play with and against assorted team members in practice until you develop an estimate of her skill level by comparison with theirs. Fit her into the ladder tentatively at an estimated position which can be revised after match play.

CHAPTER 7:
Matchmaking (Arranging Partnerships)

Now you know your team goals and have a ladder. It is time to match players with partners for doubles. Match them according to the players' skills and personalities. Here is an easy system.

Make a card for each team member with space for her name, skills, position played, court preference and partner desired. After you fill in all the information, you can easily shuffle these cards around in different combinations to come up with partnerships. Let's take the categories one by one.

Skills — Skills are what we do best in terms of strokes, running, position, attitude, etc. Match players with complimentary skills. For example, place a baseline player with a strong volleyer, a left-handed player with a right-handed, a daredevil with a conservative, etc. Each player should respect the other's complimentary skills rather than look for a partner with identical skills. Their overall skill levels need not be equal. There should not be an obvious discrepancy, though, because opponents will then focus on the weaker player exclusively.

If at all possible, the tennis coach should assist the captain in defining skill levels and strengths of players while the captain attends to the personalities. If you have no coach, you may ask all team members (assuming they know each other's games) to list the strongest points of all the others' games. The points listed most often are probably valid. For example, if five players say Myrtle has an excellent return of serve, note return of serve beside her name. Progressing through the team members, you can get a good list of outstanding skills for each.

Position Played or Ladder Level — Determine what positions each player has won in most and give her that number. For example, Nanette won most often in fifth position last season. Give her #5. Consult your ladder to get her skill level if it differs from a records ladder.

Court Preference — Find out where each player prefers to play. Does she prefer the ad or deuce side of the court or have no strong preference?

Partner Preference — Tell team members you will ask them privately to name several people they would like to play with. Ask them to consider these questions about possible partners:

- How much conversation do they like while playing?
- How much verbal direction do they like while playing?
- Do they want to take extra lessons together?
- Are they reliable?
- Are they on time?
- Are they easy going or tense?

If people already know each other and have played together, they know whether they are compatible or not. If they have not played together, do consider all the above questions. It is not necessary to be good friends to be good partners. You don't need to have anything in common but tennis.

Matchups

Now take all the cards and try to make compatible matches between them for both skills and personality. Often teams have several people with similar skill levels and records. Some may be matched with players of higher or lower skills whose personalities agree. Naturally such a combo may mean neither player plays in the position she is most familiar with. It is a good idea to explain to each player why she has been matched as she has. For example, Beatrice won in second last season and is now matched with Ermintrude who won in fourth. Together they will probably play third most of the time. They are together because they get along well. Beatrice is strong but erratic while Ermintrude is steady and accurate. Why isn't Beatrice matched with one of the players who won before in first and second positions? The reason is because none of them want to play with her. Instead they are now paired up together and will play in first and second positions.

CHAPTER 8:
Designing Lineups

So, who plays in any given week? The answer will be found in the team lineup. Make your lineups according to the team's goals discussed in Chapter 5: *What Is Our Real Goal?* This is how to make all three varieties:

Strength Lineups — Consult your ladder. Only play the most skillful each week, filling in other players in case of injury or illness in exact order of skill.

Rotation Lineups — Consult your ladder. Write a schedule in which one position changes each week in turn so that every player plays the same number of times per year.

Compromise Lineups — There are many different plans. Here are some of them:

a. Leave the top two or three positions for the same strongest players every week while rotating all the other players equally in the lower positions.

b. If you have two pairs who seem equally skilled, they can take turns playing the same position.

c. Substitutes — Do not change the entire lineup in case of illness, absence, etc. Use substitutes individually in positions commensurate with their skills to fill gaps. This gives subs a reason to stay on a large team. It is important to keep subs to avoid forfeiting.

d. Alternate several lineups depending on the opposition you face that week. First figure out what your team's strongest lineup is, next strongest, etc. Then figure out which are your strongest, next strongest, etc. opposition teams. Match your lineup to the expected strength level of the opposition rather than the calendar or number of times played. If this is the first time you face these opposition teams, you can only guess at their strength unless you can find their prior season records or do some scouting. In most leagues the teams play against each other several times. So, assuming you know nothing about your opponents in the first round of the season, schedule your lineups from strongest to weakest. By the second round you can rank your opposition. Now you know how well they played against your various strength lineups and how they did in the division (from league standings). Make a ladder of strength for those opposition teams. From now on you schedule your strongest lineups against your strongest opposition teams, middle strength lineups against middle strength opposition teams, etc.

Revisions — You will need to change your team ladder and lineups if partnerships change, players lose too often or new players join. Make sure the changes accurately reflect record (win-loss) results. To add a new player in midseason place her in a lineup one position below what the original team members at her ladder level usually play.

For example, Bernadette is new. In play against her own team members she seems to have skills equal to those of Dorcas and Cordelia. They usually play in position #2. Place her in position #3 for her first match. The reason she plays the first match one position below ladder position is because the circumstances of competition are new to her so that she is at a disadvantage. If she wins, reassign her to a higher lineup position.

CHAPTER 9:
Planning For The Future

There is a way to plan for a team that will improve each season without losing its faithful players. Decide on a set number of "regular" players. These are the people who will be part of the scheduled lineups whether they are strength, rotation or compromises. Any additional members beyond that number are called substitutes. Don't schedule subs to play normally. If, however, a regular member leaves the team due to illness, injury, travel, pregnancy, etc., a sub takes her place and becomes a regular member.

The team must decide in advance how many weeks a regular member can be absent before she loses regular status. Choose the most skilled substitute to advance into the empty regular position. Do not choose the one who has longevity. In this way more and more skilled members will fill the regular slots. Faithful and persistent members with weaker skills will not lose their places unless they leave the team for an extended period.

Part Three:
If It Weren't For The Personalities

The common theme of this section is the personality because that's what's involved in all our relationships with facilities, coaches, partners, teammates and ourselves. Anyone who plays team tennis hears the phrase, "If it weren't for the personalities," usually delivered with a sigh. Some people conclude that the word personality just means problems. Actually our personalities are what make team tennis fun. Without the highs and lows human personalities generate we'd be left with boredom. Even singles matches involve displays of personality. So, memorize the Final Four and jump right into the relationship maze with the rest of us.

What on earth are the Final Four aside from basketball? It's a list of four ultimate solutions for any and all team tennis problems. When every other attempt fails to solve your problem, these four are left. That's why they are called final:

1. Bide your time till the problem disappears.
2. Rearrange your team to suit your needs.
3. Recruit new members to rearrange the team.
4. Quit the team; move on to another team.

We have devoted separate chapters to our relationships with facilities, coaches, partners, teammates and ourselves.

217

CHAPTER 10
Relationships With Clubs And Facilities

If you are starting a new team, try to establish good relations with your club management immediately. Point out that teams will bring prospective new members to the facility when other teams come to compete. Teams attract new members who will only join facilities which have teams. They will also bring increased income to the tennis pros for lessons, clinics and equipment. Teams bring increased revenue to the restaurants and concessions at the club.

Make sure the club management understands all the requirements before agreeing to host teams. A facility needs to provide:

1. A certain number of courts at specific times.
2. Seating for spectators and provisions for serving food.
3. Adequate, clean bathrooms.
4. Convenient drinking water and ice.
5. Lighting for night leagues.
6. Parking space.

Written Agreements

Written agreements with the club or facility are better than verbal agreements because they don't depend on memory. Write up an agreement that covers all of the above areas, plus the relationship of the team to the tennis pro. Will your team be required to use only pros hired by the facility? May you hire your own coach? (see *Clinic Problems* in Chapter 11). If you use the club's tennis pro, what will his or her duties be regarding the administration of the team as opposed to the captain's duties? (see *Tennis Team Coach Services* in Chapter 11). Will the pro assign players to the teams or will they recruit their own players?

The easiest thing to do is to decide as a team what you want your relationship to be with the management. Then go to the appropriate administrator and present your ideas. Discuss them until you reach agreement. Then send your proposed agreement in the form of a letter to your club management. In it request that they notify you if they do not agree with any part of it. In lieu of negative notification, your team may consider you have a positive response.

Practical Arrangements

The following suggestions should be considered in your practical arrangements with your club management:

1. Give them a match schedule as soon as possible. Check and recheck to see that your courts have been reserved for home matches.
2. Follow the chain of command at the club. For example, if the pro's job is to reserve courts, talk to him or her; if it is someone else's, talk to her.

3. Do your best to reserve courts away from social players and unrelated clinics.
4. Make sure there are enough courts to accomodate team play and still leave courts for non-team club members. If at all possible, there should be two more courts than the number required for a home match.

Problems and Solutions

Management — Even though your agreement with a club will prevent most conflicts, outbreaks of discontent may still occur. Also, many of us are on established teams which have never had a written agreement with our facilities. Sometimes a new administrator decides to dictate new rules over established team rules. An example is the case where Barbara, a relatively new member of a facility, announces that she is entitled to play on a particular team because she pays the same club dues as the other team members. The team says Barbara may not join their team because they already have a full membership or Barbara does not meet the skill levels of their team or Barbara refuses to follow team rules. The unwary administrator informs the captain that they must accept Barbara. If you have a written agreement with a club about new team members, bring it to the attention of the new administrator. If not, the entire team may vote to move to another facility minus Barbara. Unfortunately this scenario actually happens from time to time when club management interferes with well established teams. Fortunately, most club managers do not want to assume the weekly administrative responsibility of actually running a tennis team so they wisely avoid interference with team management. Remember, tennis teams are blessings to facilities, not the other way around.

Physical Design of Facility — Prevent ball bedlam! Some facilities have several courts adjacent to each other without separating fences. During matches balls roll from court to court. Sometimes the balls on separate courts bear identical numbers. Soon the players shift their focus from tennis to ball bedlam. A local team captain, Susan Smith, devised a brilliant solution for her home matches. She assigns one person to buy all the balls for a particular match. This member buys five cans of balls with consecutive numbers on them—one can with balls marked #1, one can with #2, one can with #3, one can with #4, and one can with #5. Since balls now come in see through containers, we can easily read the numbers on them. On match day you can assign the ball numbers to the correspondingly numbered court (#1 balls on court #1 etc.) or assign the ball numbers to the corresponding lineup position (give #1 balls to #1 lineup position players, etc.).

CHAPTER 11:
Relationships With Tennis Professionals

Tennis Pro Or Team Coach?

Our teams need lessons from tennis professionals to help improve our skills. Does your team want a coach as well as a tennis pro? Look at the difference between them:

A tennis professional is a person who is paid to teach tennis. The younger tennis professionals have often passed tests given by the United States Professional Tennis Association to certify their teaching skills. Older pros may not have such credentials but have fine reputations in their communities for their teaching skills.

A tennis team coach is a tennis pro who also provides some or all of the following services in addition to teaching:

1. Partnership arrangement advice
2. Observation of matches between team members
3. Observation of league matches
4. Pre/post match advice
5. Lineup arrangement advice
6. Evaluation of player's strengths
7. Pregame strategy, peptalks, etc.

No matter how skillful our team members are, we cannot be as objective as a nonmember in advising the team. All professional sports teams have coaches. None of them expect their team captains to perform coaching duties. It may be difficult but do try your best to find a coach. If you do not find one, make the best possible use of your tennis pro (see *Maximizing Clinic Benefits*).

Hiring A Coach Or Pro

Find out what your team wants from a pro or coach before you talk to one. Be specific about the duties they want the pro to perform. Find out how much they are willing to pay for his or her services. Contact prospective tennis pros or coaches and convey the above information. Come to an agreement regarding duties and price. Depending on what she or he agrees to do, you know whether you have a tennis pro or a coach or both.

Clinic Possibilities

Here are activities to choose from during clinics:

- Drills for specific strokes, shots, placement, etc.
- Correction of individual styles and/or strokes
- Observation of matches between team members for correction of improper court position, strategy, etc.
- Evaluation of player strengths
- Pre-match strategic planning
- Physical conditioning work

Maximizing Clinic Benefits

These are suggestions for the model clinic participant:

1. Pay promptly and efficiently. Set up a system in advance for collecting money and be ready to pay. Don't waste clinic time collecting money, making change, discussing bookkeeping, etc. Make one person responsible for financial dealings (see *Treasurer* in Chapter 3 under *Who's In Charge Here*).
2. Listen while the instructor talks to you.
3. Ask questions, no matter how basic they may seem, or how many other people seem to know the answers.
4. If your coach is willing to observe you in actual match play, seize this opportunity. How can we actually expect accurate assessments of our play by people who have never seen us in actual game situations? You can get over your nervousness when your coach watches you. We overcome our anxiety during official matches by repetition. We can overcome "coach anxiety" the same way.

The Qualities Of The Ideal Coach

She or he

- gives players honest feedback regarding their tennis skill,
- tells players to concentrate on specific areas,
- gets to know the team members,
- works with what is available. In other words, she or he can suggest creative ways to use players with major gaps in their skills, lack of physical conditioning, etc.
- tries to impart wisdom learned from competitive play,
- teaches at an appropriate level for the players' skills,
- never humiliates players,
- does not allow reinforcement of mistakes,
- can keep large numbers of players busy during drills,
- does not have "teacher's pets."

Clinic Problems and Solutions

These are the common problems that confound clinics and solutions for them:

Noise Pollution — Everybody is talking. Nobody listens to the instructor. Discuss it at a team meeting. Find out why the team is talking so much. Is it because you are not active enough? If you were, you would be out of breath. Is it because your team doesn't know how to behave at clinics? Our conversation comes free of charge, but the pro's words do not. All this chitchat is a waste of our investment. Is it because you are bored? What would you rather be doing? Work with your pro to make the clinics more interesting. Maybe your team talks too much because it doesn't want clinics at all. In any case, find out what the reason for the problem and address that.

Clinic Allergy — Some members don't want to take any lessons. If the majority wants clinics, then they will either go along or quit the team if the clinics are mandatory. Teams may vote to exempt those people, but if they do, resentment will follow.

Practice Passion — Some members would rather have practice matches than clinics. Discuss and vote among these ideas:

1. Alternate clinics and practice matches.
2. Have practices another day in addition to clinic days.
3. Suggest those members quit the team for one that doesn't have clinics.
4. Exempt them from clinics and let them set up separate practice matches.
5. Abandon clinics in favor of practices.

Individual Tennis Pro Aversion — One team member has a personality conflict with the coach. Possible solutions are numbers three and four above or she can try to tolerate the pro until the majority decides to change coaches.

Mass Tennis Pro Aversion — Several members dislike the coach or the clinics. Discuss in team meeting and think of ways the specific deficiencies might be remedied. The captain or spokesperson then talks to the pro to seek change. If this scenario occurs repeatedly, it is probably time for a new coach.

Unequal Time — A player complains that the coach spent too much time with the other players and not enough with her. First find out if this is true. Then see if it happens again. If it does, speak to the coach about better time management. If it is not true or the same player complains of lack of attention repeatedly, it probably reflects that player's needs for a disproportionate amount of attention. Since this problem lies with the player's personality, no coach can remedy it without neglecting the other team members. This matter should be brought up in a team meeting so the player can see that her perception differs from the majority. She can then try to adjust her perception, quit the team, convince the team to exempt her from clinics or convince the team to eliminate clinics.

Coaching Monopoly — Your team dislikes your facility's tennis pro intensely but the management will not allow any other pro to give clinics at the facility. Discuss this at a team meeting. Find out if the team is willing to travel elsewhere to take clinics. If the team is willing to travel, begin the search for a new coach elsewhere. If the team is not willing to travel for clinics, members who want clinics (probably a majority) will probably need to join other teams. Meet with club management. Explain that the team refuses to take clinics from the club pro. Point out that your team will either leave on clinic days or break up altogether. In either case the facility will lose revenue. Suggest they work out a financial arrangement with another pro to give clinics to your team at your facility. If you can't reach agreement with the management, travel for clinics. If team members won't travel, they may join new teams separately. Or perhaps your entire team will decide to move to a different facility.

CHAPTER 12:
Relations With Partners

During competition tension rises and our public masks fall away. That is why tennis partnerships become so intense. Your relationship with your tennis partner tells the world how you handle all your two person relationships. Let's say you let your friends and lovers mistreat you while you complain behind their backs. Unfortunately, your tennis partnership may turn out the same way. It's well worth some effort on your part to make a good partnership. Aside from friendship, a good partner can improve your game results immensely.

Basic Ingredients Of A Good Partnership

The key ingredients in a good relationship are *admiration, conflict resolution* and *assertiveness.*

Admiration — You must admire some aspect of your partner's game (for example, her serve) or her personality (for example, her sense of humor). If you do not honestly admire anything at all about her, your hostility will emerge and cause trouble.

Conflict Resolution — Conflict cannot be avoided between human beings, so arrange a way to resolve differences with your partner. Arrange your system ahead of time when you are both in good humor. Ask your partner what she wants you to say when you find yourself at odds with her. This way you will know how to phrase your complaint or objection in a way she can tolerate. Then tell her the same about yourself.

Assertiveness — Always put objections in a tactful, assertive fashion. e.g. "At the beginning of the season we agreed to take lessons together but you have never been available since then. I am afraid we won't keep up with the other women and will lose our place if we don't take some lessons." If you are not familar with assertive communication, we strongly recommend some reading or a training course. It is a wonderful skill for life. *The Assertive Woman* by Stanlee Phelps and Nancy Austin is a terrific book.

Set a time after matches to analyze your play. Start by criticizing your own game and let your partner criticize hers. Then bring up your praise and criticism of her game and let her do the same for yours. Make plans to remedy the problem areas by next match.

Read books and articles that tell you how to have better tennis partnerships. *Tennis Psychology*, pages 62-65, has some wonderful material (see Bibliography Reference #10).

Dos And Don'ts During Practices And Matches

Don't

- discuss health problems,
- complain (about weather, courts, food, balls, recent weight gain,

ungrateful children, how badly you are playing, etc.),
- berate your partner,
- throw tantrums or sulk,
- blame her when you lose,
- question line calls until you see a pattern of abuse,
- pick trivial fights with opponents,
- distract your partner with chitchat about non-tennis subjects,
- snarl, frown, sneer, groan or laugh at partner's errors,
- give up during the match,
- apologize repeatedly. She knows you aren't making errors on purpose. When she runs out of responses to your apologies, she begins to wish you would be quiet and concentrate.

Do
- discuss your strategy,
- remind your partner to take whatever props she needs to play her best game (medicine, earmuffs, water, sunscreen, etc.),
- phrase suggestions as questions, e.g., "Should we both stand back?",
- smile at your partner,
- make encouraging remarks, e.g., "We'll do better next set.",
- explain your personal idiosyncracies to your partner if she is new, e.g., "When I get ahead in score, I lose concentration; please warn me about this if we get two games ahead.",
- get to match sites early enough to help your partner warm up if she needs a longer warmup than you do,
- make yourself available for lessons and extra games,
- share the credit when you win,
- warn your partner if you'll be late to a match so she won't become a nervous wreck wondering if you've overslept, gotten lost or had an accident,
- praise her good strokes,
- tell your partner right away if you become pregnant, and ask her to reveal any objections to playing with a pregnant partner. Make an agreement with her about taking leave from match play if your play becomes impaired by your condition,
- go for all of your own balls.

Problems and Solutions

Yes, there will still be problems even if you are 99% perfect. There is no escape from them, alas! There are two pseudo-solutions to reject out of hand. They may solve the problem on one particular day, but they lead to more problems in the future. One is throwing tantrums till the thrower gets her way. The other is sulking till the sulker gets her way. In either case, the other partner becomes resentful, eventually tires of abuse and wants a different partner. On to some specific problems and solutions:

Partner Aversion — You dislike your current partner. Try to solve the specific problems by yourself. If you fail, ask for advice from a person with long and good experience in getting along with others. Try their ideas. If they fail, try to think of a different partnership arrangement for yourself. At the same time consider all the rearrangements that would be needed for the other players on the team if you get a new partner you have in mind. Present your plan to your captain and try to sell it. If she refuses to accept it, you can:

1. Join another team.
2. Stay with the current partner and hope the captain will change her mind.
3. Wait for a new player to join your team and become your partner.
4. Go out and recruit a new partner for yourself from outside your team.

Whatever you do, be discreet when you talk about your problem. If you and your partner are both unhappy with the partnership, you can pursue the above solutions jointly.

Inappropriate Matchmaking — You think your newly assigned partner is all wrong. Ask your captain to explain her reasoning to you privately. Ask her to be frank about your skills and or personality traits which influenced her choice. If you do not agree with these evaluations, politely tell her you disagree. Either wait for partners to change, propose an alternative plan for your team, bring a non-team member to be your partner or move to another team.

Sliding Downhill — Your partner's playing skills have gone downhill due to health problems. Report this to the captain. If the coach's observation and match results confirm your opinion, the captain may rearrange the ladder and the lineup to reflect the altered skill level. In other words, she may move your partner lower on the ladder and raise another person to your level to be a new partner for you. Point out to the captain that you deserve to keep your rank on the ladder and place in the lineup. Maybe she demotes you anyway with the deteriorating partner because she cannot restructure the partnerships at this time. If so, choose one of the Final Four alternatives outlined for the first two problem scenarios.

Pregnancy — This is a problem only when your partner's skills are decreasing because she is pregnant. First try prevention. The minute you know she is pregnant, ask for her intentions. Ask her what she wants you to do if you see she is not playing as well as before. If you don't want to play with a partner who may injure herself due to impaired balance, be frank with her. Be sure to hold this discussion at the beginning of the pregnancy. Later you will be too embarassed to "pick on" a pregnant woman. If she tells you to inform her frankly when her skills have declined, then it is up to you to do it. It is not right to nurse silent grievances against her because you lack courage to speak up.

Playing while pregnant does not necessarily present problems. During one season our team fielded five pregnant women. Each one adjusted differently to her physical condition. Some played beautifully up to the day of delivery. Others could not.

Miscellaneous Mischief — Your partner does any of the Don'ts previous-ly listed. Be assertive. Speak to her with I messages. For example, "Eloise, I need to speak to you. I feel so depressed when you complain about everything before our matches that I really lose the energy I need to play well. I ask you not to say anything negative till we've won at least two sets. Thank you." or "Morgana, I got so scared when you gave me that dirty look after I double faulted that I could hardly bring myself to try the serve I've been working on for months. Believe me, double faulting is very upsetting to me. I ask you not to put more pressure on me by glaring."

Assertiveness Failure — If assertive communication is not effective with your partner, it is time to retreat to the Final Four solutions:

1. Bide time.
2. Rearrange team.
3. Recruit.
4. Quit.

Absolute Integrity — Your partner did not tell the truth about events during the match. She insists that you back up her version. Your teammates tell you to show your team loyalty by backing her story. You are absolutely sure that your version is the factual one. Team loyalty does not include dishonesty. If your partner and teammates want you to lie, it is time to look for another team to join.

Summary

One of the saddest things to see in team tennis is the case of the woman no one wants to have as a partner. There really are people with extremely unpleasant behavior who absolutely cannot or will not change. We address this situation again from a captain's point of view in Chapter 18. If you are paired with such a person and the partnership fails, you are not to blame. On the other hand, you may be paired with a person who has only the usual human quota of undesirable traits. If you do nothing to assert yourself and the relationship sours, take 50% of the responsibility. Try hard to improve matters. An unlikely candidate may turn out to be your ideal tennis partner. Really!

Your own responsibilities as a good partner are covered in Chapter 14: *Relations With Yourself.*

CHAPTER 13:
Relations With Teammates

Our teammates magnify all our victories. They maximize our pride and joy when we win. Our teammates downplay all our defeats. They minimize our disappointments and sadness when we lose.

The way you relate to your teammates reflects your behavior in other groups like your family, business and social groups. The problem we face as group members is how to get our individual needs met while pursuing a group goal. In the case of our tennis teams, of course, our main goal is to play good tennis. Any individual who wants to do something which detracts from group tennis will find herself on the outs with her team.

Most women have never played on athletic teams. That is why women have trouble learning to put team goals first and personal goals second. It is not because we are women that we have conflicts within our teams. It is very sad to hear women insult themselves with such phrases as, "Well, you know how women are", or "Women just can't get along with each other." Women get along as well as any other groups of human beings. Sometimes we get along very well and have excellent teams too. Players who have been on athletic teams before or have been on tennis teams for a long time have far less difficulty than those who are new to team tennis. They have learned to be team players. Most negative conflict comes from misunderstanding our roles as team players, poor team organization, or individual behavioral problems. As we have already covered organization earlier, let's turn to behavioral problems and team roles.

Behavioral Problems

Why are some people more popular than others on their teams? Eliminate the mystery. It's quite simple. If you want to annoy your teammates, follow the directions in the first list. If you want to be liked and respected by your teammates, follow the directions in the second list.

How To Annoy Your Teammates

1. When the captain calls the night before a match to ask you to sub in an emergency to prevent forfeiting, tell her, "Sorry, I wasn't on the schedule so I made my annual complete physical appointment for tomorrow".
2. Always ask for a ride, particularly if you don't live near anyone else.
3. Come late to meetings and ask for all the information to be repeated for your benefit.
4. Never contribute your own can of new balls.
5. Play a social match on a court next to your team's practice match or clinic after telling them you are too busy to attend their practice or clinic.
6. Keep a running inventory on the whereabouts of all three balls while playing a match. e.g. "I have two. Do you have the other? Is it in the corner?" and so forth. The point of the game is to play rather than hold onto three balls from beginning to end.
7. Throw or drop the second ball behind you after serving the first ball. This is a cause for a Let call (U.S.T.A. Rule #21, Comment #2).
8. Just before you start a match tell your partner you can only play two sets because you need to leave.
9. Refuse to participate in team activities, particularly if you imply that they are silly.
10. At every team gathering insist that you have been treated differently or unfairly from everyone else.

11. Refuse to take a leave of absence when your skills have clearly deteriorated due to physical misfortune.
12. Talk continuously during meetings, practices and clinics.
13. When you lose a match, blame your partner or the lineup.
14. When it's time to pick up balls during clinics, buttonhole the tennis pro for a private conference instead.
15. Bring your children to practices or matches so they can enjoy team refreshments and get their exercise climbing the wire fences.
16. Slow down the pace of the game by sitting down every time you change ends, sauntering rather than walking, etc.

How To Delight Your Teammates

1. Be willing and happy to play with any teammate. If you are high up on the ladder, your teammates will be very grateful to you. If they should someday reach your skill level or even exceed it, you will still have friends.
2. When you have a complaint or problem, try hard to think of a solution before vocalizing.
3. Help teammates warm up when their partners aren't available.
4. Repeat only the positive remarks people make about each other. e.g. "Susie thinks your backhand is terrific." NOT, "Susie thinks you need a good weight loss program."
5. Pick up your share of tennis balls during clinics.
6. Never allow your team to forfeit a match because of you unless you are in a true emergency.
7. Volunteer to go to the match even though you are not scheduled to play. You might be needed to fill in and save your team from forfeiting.
8. If you can't keep a prearranged social match, try very hard to get your own replacement.
9. Always carry *The Code, USTA Rules*, and your league rules. Read them and try to learn them. Many so-called bad habits in social tennis are really rules violations.
10. Do not make personal appointments on days of practices or matches; you never know when your team may need you.
11. When something needs to be done for the team, volunteer to do it. Make sure, however, you don't take on too much work. It is true that most people will enjoy having you do their share but it will backfire on you. Do your share and let others do theirs.
12. Let your captain know which dates you can't come to practices, clinics or matches as soon as possible so she can make long-range plans.

Troublesome Teammates And How To Handle Them

Unfortunately, even with the best of intentions, most teams will have a few people with behavioral problems. Here are some of the most common problem players and some suggestions for getting along with them:

Hypochondriacs— They always complain of bodily ills. Their recitation of health problems can have a demoralizing effect on their partners and teams. Sometimes they will let the team down in a crunch. Handle them with polite, mild sympathy. Avoid helping them decide whether to play or not by saying "It's up to you Samantha." Don't encourage morbid conversations about symptoms; change the subject.

Complainers, Whiners and Pessimists— They can cause low team morale. Do not try to argue them out of their glum views. Meet every complaint or whine with the response, "What do you think we should do about it?" Meet pessimistic predictions with, "Yes, it might happen like that, but on the other hand it might happen like this." Then present an optimistic outcome. Any team which has more than two of these people needs to recruit new, more cheerful players.

Undercover Agitators — They stir up trouble among team members by reporting negative remarks about each other, passing false information around, and suggesting negative motives for the actions of others. When a troublemaker passes on a negative remark made about you, ask her, "Why are you telling me this? Do you want to make me unhappy?" When you hear troublemakers passing around dubious information, insist on knowing the source. Question their facts. When they suggest a negative motive for someone's actions, say "It could have been that but they also could have done it for this reason. Then give a plausible positive motive.

Tantrum Throwers— They disrupt games and change the level of excitement at matches from exhilaration to agitation. At the time of a flareup discourage them by withdrawing attention. Bring up the problem at the next team meeting. Insist on team penalties for such behavior and stick to them.

Space Cadets — These are unreliable people who can't be counted on to show up on time. They forget meetings, practices, clinics, lessons, equipment, etc. They need caretakers. If they can't follow team rules, eject them from the team or let them be substitutes. What about the player who is unreliable but follows team rules? If someone is willing to take the job, appoint a caretaker. This person can carry Space Cadet's equipment, drive her to matches, etc. Make a contingency plan in case she forgets or is late for a match; have a substitute ready!

Privileged Characters— They consider themselves more skilled than their records indicate so they are never satisfied with their lineup placement and/or caliber of partner. They also believe they are entitled to exemptions from team rules of all kinds. Remind them of the facts as shown in the match records. Consistently deny them exemptions from established team rules. Point out how their perception of their ability and placement differs from reality.

Underprivileged Characters — They have the opposite viewpoint about their skills. The mildest praise is overwhelming to them and they rebut it with self-criticism. They are emotionally draining to their partners who try fruitlessly to build their lack of self-esteem. Any position on the lineup is too high for them according to their assessment. Remind them of the facts as shown in the match records. Point out that their perception differs from reality. Do not devote large amounts of time to praising them.

Primadonnas — They are the team's best players who have lost humility. Now they have decided they deserve special rewards in the form of the best partners, extra attention from the tennis pro or exemption from clinics altogether, exemptions from team rules, and admiration and gratitude from all other team members. Express the team's gratitude to primadonnas for their skill and contribution but insist that they follow team rules. Bring up the individual's demands before the whole team. If your team is in contention for a trophy when she insists on special treatment or threatens to quit, take a team vote on what to do. If your team votes to give in to her demands, collect your trophies at the awards banquet and do not allow her to join your team next season.

Team Roles

As a team member, your role is to promote the success of the group. Whatever you do that unites the group is good; whatever you do that divides the group is bad.

Building team spirit is the way to unite a team. Chapter 17 describes in detail many ways to build team spirit. Don't leave this job for your captain. She can't do it all by herself. Read and put the new ideas to work. You're probably already using many of them if you're on an established team.

Many items on the *How To Annoy Your Teammates* list are divisive actions. Disrupting meetings with lateness and noise will definitely divide the team because it delays problem solving. Refusing to participate in team activities divides a team into inner and outer members. Granting special favors and rules exemptions divides a team into privileged and underprivileged classes. On the other hand, expressing honest disagreement is not divisive to a team. Healthy people always have some differences of opinion.

There is a team fact of life that is hard for many people to learn. The team's welfare is more important *to the team* than any individual's welfare. That's why you are bound to lose if you pit yourself against an entire team. There is nothing personal about this. It is equally true for all of us. It's just the way groups must work to survive. If you keep this fact in mind at all times, you won't be surprised when your special wants are denied in favor of group needs. As time goes on you will probably stop asking for special treatment. Chapter 14 tells you how to get your genuine needs as an individual met while remaining a good team member. Eventually you may learn to get what you want personally and also get what's best for your team at the same time. When you've reached that point, you've become what's known as a team player. It can be done!

CHAPTER 14:
Relations With Yourself

So what do we gain for ourselves from teams? After we honor our tennis facility's policies, our tennis pro's directions, our team rules, our captain's decisions and our partner's wishes, what's left for us? Fortunately we have everything to gain as individuals. We benefit directly from the exercise. We acquire new tennis skills and improve our old ones. Mastering skills steadily gives us a wonderful sense of accomplishment. We make new friends, have fun and travel. Sometimes we even win trophies. If you want to, you can learn leadership skills too, which will help you in other areas of life. There is great satisfaction in knowing that you are part of a successful group and have helped to make it successful.

How can you be sure to get the most out of team tennis for yourself? First of all you must be the one to guard your own interests. There is no one to do it for you. The captain is busy guarding the team's interests; your teammates are guarding their own interests. That leaves you to make sure you get all you can from your team experience. If you take responsibility for your own needs and refuse to allow yourself to be taken advantage of, you will enjoy team tennis. Here's how:

Do It For Your Own Sake

1. Be sure to join a compatible team. Get all the information you need before you join. Don't be afraid to ask for specific information. If a team you're considering joining seems vague about their rules and goals, beware. Either they are hiding something or they are not very well organized.

2. After you join a team, learn it's rules. Then you will know what you are supposed to be doing. You can tell if the team is sticking to them or not.

3. When you are unhappy, speak up to your partner or captain. Don't complain behind their backs. They aren't mind readers and if you don't tell them your concerns, they can't guess them.

4. Speak up at team meetings when you spot a problem; sooner or later it may get worse and affect you.

5. Guard your own health. Decide for yourself whether or not you can play if you are ill. Your teammates are probably not your personal physicians.

6. Guard your own priorities. Decide for yourself whether or not you can play if you have a conflicting commitment. Don't try to dump this decision on your partner or captain.

7. Improve your tennis skills. Take lessons, read and do whatever you need to do to improve. If you have a losing streak there is a reason for it. Don't fall into the trap of heavy philosophizing about whether or not you were meant to play tennis. Just find out what the problem is and do something about it.

8. Improve your own moods. Don't expect your partner, teammates, captain or tennis pro to spend their time praising you and cheering you up. If you have a mood disorder and/or low self-esteem, get medical evaluation and therapy.

9. Carry with you all the props you need to play well - medicines, cosmetics, extra racquets, glasses, towels, water, snacks and an extra can of balls.

10. Ask for help when you really need it. If you need a ride, daycare information, the name of a good tennis pro or doctor, ask your teammates. Shared wisdom is one of your team's greatest resources. It's all there free for you.

Abuse Prevention

To enjoy team tennis to its fullest, protect yourself from these exploitative situations:

1. Don't allow your partner to treat you in an abusive manner; make sure she understands that you will not tolerate such treatment.

2. Don't let your teammates get exemptions from team rules unless the majority votes for the exemption.

3. You are not a dump for your teammates' responsibilities. You could become very popular if you did your job and their job too, but you would eventually become exhausted and resentful.

4. Don't let your teams' needs hold back your individual progress as a tennis player. If the time comes when the team can't meet your needs for better instruction or more challenging competition, it's time for you to move to another team. Yes, it can be painful to leave your friends behind. If they are true friends, they will be happy for you.

5. You need to enjoy your tennis experiences. If there is no way the team can provide a compatible partner for you, recruit one for yourself or move to another team. Naturally, we refer to a long term situation here, not a matter of months or weeks.

Keeping Your Head Up When Your Feet Are On The Bottom Rung Of The Ladder

In every group there are different ways to achieve status. The most skillful tennis players on a tennis team automatically have the highest status. Lots of people join tennis teams who are accustomed to having a high rank in their other groups (work, family, school, volunteer organizations, social clubs). Suddenly they find themselves on the middle or even on the low rungs of their team ladders and their status plunges. This change in status can be very hard to adjust to. You can choose a negative or a positive response to this situation.

Some negative reactions to loss of status sound like this: "Well these people simply don't recognize how important I am so I'll tell them." (arrogance), or, "If I can't be on top, I'm nothing at all." (depression), or, "I know I am one of the best tennis players no matter what the ladder says." (denial of reality).

A positive way to look at this situation is to say to yourself, "Well, ok, I can't be a top dog in this pack, but I'm going to have fun anyway. I will focus on improving my own skills instead of comparing myself to other people. Inside, I know I am a fine person no matter how mediocre or awful my tennis game may be." It's also useful to remind yourself occasionally that in the whole scheme of life, tennis is only a small part. This will help to give you some perspective on your status on the tennis team.

Obviously those who take a positive approach are going to enjoy life on a tennis team much more. They can fit tennis into an appropriate part of a well-balanced life. They know that being a great tennis player doesn't make you a great person. To our knowledge Mother Theresa doesn't play tennis at all. What do you really think of yourself as a person? That's what truly matters.

PART FOUR:
First Aid Kit For The Captain

A team captain can burn out easily. We don't want that to happen to you. That's why we designed this section just for you captains. You need specific information on management, record keeping, telephones, perks, orientation, team size, team spirit, personalities and practice sessions. It's all here and it's time tested.

CHAPTER 15:
Daily Affairs

Management Style (Hilary Hitler vs. Dora Doormat)

Don't be a dictator unless you want a short, miserable reign. Do you remember why we Americans fought the Revolutionary War? We have the same independent spirit today. Your goal as captain is to manage the team so that it runs smoothly and fairly. Do not confuse this role with that of mother, teacher, employer or any other authoritarian position. You are equal in rank with your team members. On the other hand you are not a paid employee, slave, policewoman, or psychiatrist for your team members. Be on guard at all times to avoid either extreme.

If you don't like people in general and your teammates in particular, please don't take this job. They will quickly see that you don't care about them and they will not be motivated to cooperate.

Maybe human relationships just aren't that easy for you. Make an effort to get to know the members of your team on a personal level beyond their tennis roles. It is hard not to like someone when you get to know them. If you know that some of your team members do not like you and never wanted you to be their captain, make a special effort to befriend them. Often captains find that they need to spend time alone with certain team members to learn about them. In our busy lives people appreciate time spent with them more than anything else. Note your team members' special talents and commend them in public.

You must try to keep your team organized. Lack of structure wastes time and causes people to feel insecure. If you want results you must tell the members what is expected of them. That is why it is important to run good meetings and have consistently enforced written team rules.

To avoid becoming tired out, delegate extensively. Elect officers, appoint committees and don't leap to do chores other people could easily do. Make sure your co-captain or another member can take over in case of emergency. Train this person. If an emergency arises it is a great relief to know your co-captain can perform all your duties with ease.

Be as open with teammates as possible. Be frank but tactful in relaying information about skill levels and personality problems. Do not evade issues. People's imaginations will concoct more troublesome ideas with half-truths and innuendos than with the facts. There is no point in pretending the lineups have come from mysterious, other-worldly sources. You know and they know who writes them, so why not explain the reasoning behind the lineups? We don't suggest you spend hours with each member each week explaining every detail of your thinking behind the lineup. If the lineup is radically different, however, the affected players are going to wonder why.

Along the same lines, if you cannot tolerate criticism, do not become a captain. People who ask hard questions and challenge your ideas are not your enemies. Always remember that they may be right or have a valid point. As long as objections are open you have a chance to defend your ideas. As soon as ideas are not welcome, they go underground where you cannot defend your point of view.

If you begin to have trouble with your team, ask yourself honestly what the problem is. If you don't know, ask well-liked team members with good common sense. Question your own behaviors. Do all of your plans work as you hope they will or do some of them really fall flat? When you make mistakes, admit them. Flexibility is very important. If something does not work, change it.

Try to learn the *U.S.T.A. Rules*, *The Code* and your league rules well. You told your teammates to learn them and carry them to matches. If they do it, they won't disrupt your matches as much. But you must provide a good example before they will take you seriously. Sometimes there's a heated controversy during a match. You just can't find the rule or Code section you need to back up your argument. Carry a copy of *Tennis Disputes* with you. It will tell you exactly where to look. This book is an indispensable guide for settling disputes (see Bibliography Reference #2).

Record Keeping

Keep good records for your team. They will help you make better lineups. Have them on hand at all times to show the members why you do what you do. It is hard for members to complain about their respective placements when the figures are before them in black and white. You will find the following kinds of records very useful:

1. Attendance at clinics and practices. Also use these sheets to note dates when various players will not be available.
2. Match Results and Position Played. Note dates when players will not be available for matches. Write a lineup position number into the match date space for each player.
3. Percentages. From the Match/Position sheets compute the win/loss record for each player in each position. Compute the win/loss record for each partnership.

Watch records to see how the team plays against particular opponents. Report any outstanding records at team meetings. Note which partnerships are so successful they need to move up the ladder. Note which partnerships are in trouble. Records will help you deal with players who want to play in one position of the lineup. Show them their percentages in all lineup positions. Most people like the position where they win. Some teams keep their records on computers.

The Telephone, Friend or Foe?

The telephone can become your enemy if you let it. The best way to prevent this problem is to buy an answering machine. This miraculous device will save you from interrupted dinners, TV programs, and romantic interludes. It allows you to gather your wits and ammunition before discussing issues with emotionally overheated players. The answering machine helps your teammates because they can just call once and leave you a message instead of dialing your number over and over. When people know you have a machine they usually condense their thoughts into brief messages instead of babbling on and on. And finally the answering machine minimizes any jealousy your housemate may have of your teammates since it helps you control your own time.

Get a separate phone line if possible so that when your line rings it will be clear the call is for you and your family's business will not be disrupted by tennis calls. If you cannot install a separate line, anticipate and arrange a telephone use compromise with your housemates.

Organize your team efficiently so that members will not need to call you constantly for information. Try to handle complaints and problems at team meetings. Let players know you expect to hear some solutions too and they will make fewer complaining calls. Set up a telephone chain for your team to get information to everyone in a hurry. That way if a match is cancelled because of freezing temperatures and ten players need to be informed within one half hour, it can be done easily.

Perks

Don't grab the highest spot in the lineup, the best partner on the team, and the most playing time because you are the captain. Your teammates will catch on fast and probably throw a revolution or a sit-down strike. On the other hand, don't take the lowest place on the lineup, the worst partner, and the least amount of playing time. Everyone would love you for your martyrdom but you will lose respect for yourself. Soon you'll resent them. Try to look at yourself as objectively as any other player and place yourself accordingly. Remember those written records? Use them.

Orientation

Orient your new team members well. Be sure they know the bad news about your team as well as the good. The sooner they feel comfortable on the team, the sooner they will relax and play their best games. Don't assume they know everything because they have played on teams before. The rules of their former teams may differ radically from your team customs. It will be much easier on you and kinder to them to correct misunderstandings in advance.

Retirement

Plan to phase yourself out as captain eventually. There is life for you outside this office, believe it or not. Your team members deserve a chance to learn the skills you are learning as captain. After you retire, let your successor do her job without your interference. Be willing to answer questions for her but wait to be asked.

CHAPTER 16:
Team Size

Bigger Really Is Better

How many players should a team have? Try to get as many players on your team as your league allows. The benefits of having a large roster are many:

1. The team's chances of forfeiting matches for lack of players will be minimized.
2. The addition of more players will introduce fresh thinking to the group and will sustain interest.
3. The members won't become lazy because they know they need to maintain their skills or slip down the ladder and/or be replaced.

Before accepting more than the basic minimum of players, explain the team's lineup policy to possible recruits. Warn them they may never get to play a match. Tell them under what conditions they will get to play a match. This will prevent later dissatisfaction due to misunderstanding. They will join with their eyes open or go elsewhere.

It is not true that people won't join a team if they think they may not play competitively. There are many incentives for joining a large team. Members receive introductions to numerous other women who will be looking for games on non-team days. Talented prospects know the team will want them to play eventually in order to win points. Aside from matchplay, team membership is still a social opportunity, particularly for those new to an area. If players are new to tennis altogether, a big team gives them more time to build up courage before being thrown into real competition. Team membership gives people access to clinics which cost less than private lessons. It's easier to set up practice matches when there are more players. It's easier to shuffle partnerships around when there are numerous combinations.

On smaller teams the players play more often. There is less record keeping and organizing for the captain. Some tiny teams skip meetings altogether. When a team is too small it can become impossible to shift partners around. Constant fear of forfeiting causes stress.

Odd Numbers

Having an odd number of members on a team which plays doubles presents organizational challenges. Here are some solutions:

1. If a person in the middle of your ladder loses a partner, give her a new one from another partnership, change the other partnership as needed and leave the single person to be a substitute.
2. Ask someone to volunteer to sub and then realign all the partnerships.
3. Give a person who plays third position no fixed partner and let her play with alternate members who are qualified by their records to play third position.
4. Put the single player with a partnership at third position to form a triad, one of whom will sit out each time they are scheduled to play.

CHAPTER 17:
Building Team Spirit

What Is It?

Team spirit is a mind set held by all members of the team that they are united for a common purpose. An example of this spirit occurs when team members come out to watch their team matches even though they are not scheduled to play. On many teams players on the lower end of the ladder have voluntarily given up their lineup spots long enough to let better players win points needed to give the entire team a coveted trophy. Sometimes a team member with an outstanding stroke will donate her time to drill other members.

Here is an example of team spirit from our team. A second position player's babysitting arrangement fell through at the last minute on match day. Even though a third position player could have substituted, she knew that she wasn't as likely to win. Instead of insisting on playing, she graciously offered to babysit. The second position player played the match and won. It's worth building team spirit to minimize internal dissension and maximize enjoyment. It will be much easier for the captain to manage a group with good team spirit.

Where Do We Find Some?

The real question is how do you build team spirit? First of all, in any discussion, shift the focus from the individual's gain or loss to the team's gain or loss. When individuals confront you with requests for favors, improved status, etc., tell them their requests will be seriously considered in light of overall group gain because the team takes precedence. This message must be conveyed at the very beginning and repeated throughout the season. It must be related to new members as part of their orientation. For example, Josephine requests permission to go to a great sale on designer pantyhose instead of attending her team's weekly practice session. She says she can play in the match anyway. As captain, you respond to Josephine that she may not play in the match because it is a team rule that team members must attend the weekly practice session in order to play in that week's match. If you make an exception for her pantyhose sale, the other 15 team members might want to attend sales all over the county and soon team practice would not exist.

Everybody on the team must believe she belongs before she will have any team spirit. Make it clear to substitutes and less skilled players that their contribution is vital even if they aren't playing as many matches. Be specific about their contributions in front of the other team members.

Encourage anything which will bond your group. Examples are uniforms, parties and trips. These things may seem trivial to a serious athlete. They are not essential to improving tennis skills, that's true. But they are essential to building and maintaining team spirit. The time a group spends building bonds of friendship is just as important to their success as a group as the time they spend building skills. Research confirms this.

Discourage the formation of cliques. Explain at the beginning of the season how important team spirit is. Make everyone feel welcome. Be a good example yourself by speaking to everyone, sitting with different people at meals, and riding with different groups to matches. Do not hold whispered conferences with small subgroups in front of other team members.

Publicize the activities of your team in club and league newsletters, and on bulletin boards. Speak enthusiastically about your team. Enthusiasm is contagious. Encourage a spirit of us (our team) versus them (opposition teams) by updating the standings, and sharing information about other teams.

By now you know there is much more to running a good team than simply winning matches. We know there are teams whose members don't like each other. Some don't even know each other. They may have no grasp of basic league information either and still have excellent scores. But they miss a major reason for team play which is to be part of a group. Their experience when they go to collect a trophy is very different from one where members have worked with and encouraged each other, sometimes for years.

*C*HAPTER 18:
Problematic People

How can you arrange matters so you spend as little time as possible dealing with behavior problems on the team? First let's look at general problem prevention. Then we'll deal with the player who can't control herself at matches. Last we'll examine the nightmare of every team, the player no one wants to be partners with.

Crisis Prevention

Organization plays a major part in avoiding personality problems. Players who know they have some power (their votes), some respect, and a forum for their opinions are less likely to become resentful and act up out of frustration. On the other hand, there is no question that certain people behave unpleasantly no matter how nicely they are treated.

Ideally, you will not encourage people with behavior problems to join your team. You ask your current members not to introduce such people. How do you tell about a prospective member's behavior? If she has changed teams often, this may be a clue that she does not get along well with people. It may also mean that she is very ambitious about her tennis. Such a player changes teams strictly to gain higher lineup positions, maximum playing time and more challenging competition or clinics. She may be a delightful member of your team. If a prospective member has lived in the same community for a few years and has severe behavior problems, her reputation will precede her. If a person is brand new, be aware of your own instinctual reaction but give her the benefit of the doubt.

Team Traumas

Two behavior problems may disrupt a team completely. We call them *Matchplay Fireworks* and the *Ugly Duckling*. The captain must deal with them quickly and forcefully. Be prepared!

Matchplay Fireworks — What about the player who behaves tolerably enough with your own team but seems to lose control under the stress of competition? She throws tantrums during official matches. Very often a league itself will have rules for proper behavior during matches and will discipline an errant player accordingly. On the other hand you may be part of a league where the captains are called to the scene to solve disputes. There you find your team member screaming, throwing her racquet, or using abusive language. The best thing to do in the short run is to get her attention by using her name. Draw her away from the public scene so you can talk to her. Ask her what the problem is and listen until she calms down. Ask her if she feels able to continue the match. Of course this may have used up so much time that you have now had to forfeit the match. Tell her you and the other captain will make a ruling and do so. After the match tell her you will discuss her behavior at the next team meeting. Decide as a team what to do about it.

This is a good example of why teams should set up rules in advance of unpleasant events. If your team has already set up a rule with consequences for unsportsmanlike behavior, she knows what the results will be. It is very important to stand up to abusive people firmly. Their behavior becomes worse if you do not confront them.

The Ugly Duckling — One of your players has had numerous partners. Each one made a noble effort to get along with her. Everyone deserted her eventually. Now what can you do with this ostracized individual? Have a private conversation with her. Explain the problem, e.g., "I can't figure out how to make a good partnership for you. You have been with A, B, and C and could not get along with any of them. What do you suggest now?" If she suggests the name of a person who is willing to try her, your problem is solved temporarily. If she suggests someone who is not a possibility, you must tell her that idea won't work. Ask for another suggestion ad infinitum until all members' names are exhausted. If no one will be partners with her, tell her the bad news. Inform her that you do not have the power to force anyone to play with her.

Suppose your team has so few players you can't afford to lose this player. After you reach the point where no one will agree to be her regular partner, tell her you will ask the team members if they will take turns playing with her at an appropriate level for her skills. When the reason for this idea, that is no players, no points, is explained to the team members, they will probably agree to play alternate matches with her as a partner. If your team members would rather lose points than play tennis with the difficult individual, that is their decision to make. If you know of any team with a small roster, give her the name of their captain.

What if this "ugly duckling" is totally blameless, an unfortunate victim of a malicious team? That would certainly be a tragedy. We have never heard of such a situation in real life. In all the cases we have heard of, an ostracized individual has repeated her unacceptable behavior so often that each of her team members lost their tolerance. Normally we have a great deal of sympathy for the underdog. We lose our sympathy only after tolerating outrageous behavior for a prolonged period.

It is unfortunate that our affairs can become so brutal but it is only natural. No part of our society is constantly peaceful and harmonious. There is no reason to think tennis teams would be any exception. Maybe we are surprised because we persist in believing that, "It's only a game." Games call up the competitive spirit we need for survival. Team membership also increases our intensity. Belonging to a team means belonging to a group. For our ancestors, group membership meant survival; a human being was too weak to live alone. So even though we're walking upright and wearing attractive uniforms as well, we're still very intense about our groups.

When you accept a position as captain, prepare yourself to deal with behavior problems. If you honestly think you can't handle them or hate the idea of it, do not become a team captain. Did you notice, by the way, that there's no advice here about solving your team members' personal problems with lengthy sessions on the telephone or visits? The reason is because psychotherapy is not a duty of a team captain. Even if you are trained as a therapist, you can't be objective toward your own team members. If they need psychotherapy, they deserve better therapy than you can deliver as a sideline.

CHAPTER 19:
Practice Sessions

Arrangements

If you are arranging practice sessions without the help of a tennis pro, there are several formats to choose from:

1. Play regular matches against each other.
2. Play a specified number of round-robin games against each other.
3. Get ideas for drills from tennis books and your coach and use them.

If you want to play matches among team members but not stay on the same courts all session, you can ask the winners of the first round to play each other and the losers to play each other. If you want matches to be shorter and end at about the same time, play a predetermined number of no-ad games.

If you want to play round-robins, there are carefully worked out charts for arranging assorted numbers of players. A good sourcebook for these charts is Eleanor Owens' book, *Tennis: Easy On - Easy Off* (see Bibliography Reference #16.) Your tennis facility may also keep copies of round-robin charts. The charts assign each player a number. One method for assigning numbers is to sign each name in order of arrival at the courts along side a number on a sheet of paper.

Another way is to use a set of playing cards. Take the same number of cards as there are players. Make sure there are four of each kind, e.g. four aces, four 2s, etc. Ask each player to draw a card. Instruct holders of black suit cards to play as partners against holders of red suit cards. e.g. Players with ten of Spades and ten of Clubs play as partners against players with ten of Hearts and ten of Diamonds. Players draw cards again after each predetermined number of games is complete.

Problems and Solutions

Here are some common problems which plague practices and suggestions for dealing with them:

Boredom — No matter how good a practice idea is, it will get stale eventually. Change the format. If you are pre-season you could invite another club to play with your team or ask another team at your own club to play with you. Do something different.

Competition — The purpose of the practice is to improve the skills of all the players and bring them together rather than drive them apart. Repeat over and over that this is the time to experiment. Try those new shots and strategies. Ask your opponents to tell you which of your shots were most effective. Practice your serve. The purpose is not to humiliate your teammates with your great scores. If you have superstars on your team, the other members may not want to play with them, claiming it's useless. Remind them that they can use the opportunity to prepare for similar overwhelming opposition in real matches. Perhaps they can even try some outlandish strategies since there is nothing to lose.

Uneven Numbers — There is no perfect solution to this dilemma. Don't spend excessive time trying to ensure an even number of players at every practice. You could spend hours arranging even numbers only to have someone fall ill the morning of the practice. You will have more than enough to do as you make sure you have the required number of players at the official matches. It is important, however, to discourage players from going home or sitting in a chair when they are extra. A threesome can always do drills or play Australian. An individual can take a bucket of balls and practice her serve. One local captain, Maggie Cosmillo, has a successful tip to minimize both the superstar's boredom and the uneven number problem. She invites players from a higher division team to come to her team practices. The higher level players provide novelty, strong competition for her team's highest players and they also sub for absentees. You may want to borrow this super suggestion.

PART FIVE:
Ad-Ons

Some vital information doesn't fit into the other categories. We added it on here. Gift suggestions might save you hours of indecision or even embarrassment. Information on uniforms will protect you from expensive mistakes. By now you know we favor problem prevention. That's why we've included advice for new players and rules of etiquette and safety. We want you to make friends and avoid hurt feelings while you stay healthy.

CHAPTER 20:
Gift Ideas For Banquets, Parties and Holiday Exchanges

We gathered these ideas from reactions to gifts at parties and banquets over the years. Certain gifts were always popular. Those are the ones on our first two lists.

Tennis Themed Treasures:

- Tennis Balls
- Drink Containers
- Collages of Team Photos
- Wrist Bands
- Special Shoe Laces
- Albums of Team Photos
- Trophies - Funny or Serious
- Clothing - only if you know the recipient's taste and size and it can be exchanged.
- Tennis Towels - particularly with team or players' names or initials.
- Gift Certificates - for tennis/sporting goods stores.
- Stationery - cards and paper. One source of clever cards including holiday cards is Sportcards, P.O. Box 817, Newport, RI 02840.

- Jewelry - If you know the recipient's taste. It must be of excellent quality; a corroded piece will leave bad memories.
- Coffee Mugs - with team or players' names and/or titles and dates.

You may buy these treasures at tennis stores, pro shops, sporting goods emporiums and gift shops.

Non-Tennis Gifts:

- Potpourri
- Picture Frames
- Photo Albums - engraved or embossed
- Padded and/or Scented Hangers
- Christmas Tree Decorations
- Movie Gift Certificates
- Food and Wine Baskets
- Restaurant Gift Certificates
- Engraved Silver Plate Serving Pieces
- Additions to the recipient's personal collections if you know her current holdings.
- Clothing or Home Decor Items - only if you know the recipient's taste and the items are exchangeable.

Absolute No-Nos:

- Tennis Racquets - They must meet the players' personal tastes. Most people like to try them out first before purchasing.
- Tennis Equipment Bags - These have the same drawbacks as the racquets. People are particular about size, color, etc.
- Cute or Clever Items - These are objects of questionable taste. What one person thinks is cute may be considered awful by others. How about a ceramic duck with a fabric bonnet on its downy head? Some women may long to own one. Other will draw back in horror. If you can't tell whether an item is supposed to be a joke gift or not, don't buy it as a sincere tribute.

CHAPTER 21:
Uniforms

The purpose of uniforms is to help blend a collection of individuals into a team. They also give us the message that we are now dressed for serious competition, as opposed to just fooling around.

‚ to select uniforms, the team should choose two members
mittee. Two people will be able to give each other company
‚ work. Efficiency will decline if there are more than two.
‚e asks team members for their ideas about style, fabric and
 me factors to consider:

1. *Appearance.* If you look good, you feel better. Most teams prefer a sleek athletic look; no cutey-pies or sex-kittens, please.
2. *Durability.* Bright and dark colors may fade. Some polyester blends pill up quickly.
3. *Comfort.* How comfortable will you be in both heat and cold extremes? You will need to add and subtract layers without completely undressing. Are sleeve openings and shoulders large enough to allow for big serves? Make sure pockets are deep enough to hold an extra ball.
4. *Expense.* Not everyone wishes to purchase an expensive uniform. If you want to save money, you can all wear identical t-shirts. Some companies will sell custom designed shirts at reasonable prices.
5. *Care.* Few team tennis players want to iron uniforms or take their gear to the drycleaner.
6. *Availability.* Tennis specialty stores can order team uniforms directly from national manufacturers. They will probably offer a team discount for a big order. Unfortunately it takes time to get the uniforms and the date of delivery is not always dependable. Naturally, the more clothing you can find already in stock, the better.
7. *Colors.* Dark ones are too warm in hot climates. Red is powerful psychologically, but it looks hot and may fade. It's not possible to match every person's color chart, so, some must dress out of season. Bandannas around the neck can minimize the effects of an out of season color.

After the team decides on general uniform ideas, the committee researches local stores. Committee members choose about three possible styles from what is available. Then they present these to the team for a vote. Sources of clothing are tennis shops, pro shops or team sports stores. The latter can design logos for your uniforms. Sporting goods stores and department stores may not have enough of any one style or color in stock for all the different sizes you'll need.

CHAPTER 22:
News For New Players

Too often, new players get their feelings hurt or become angry because nobody warned them about the unwritten facts of tennis life. Know what to expect from tennis players, team tennis and/or your new team.

Beginners

1. Better players don't really want to play with you. This does not mean you are not a wonderful person. They don't want to play with you because a match would be too easy. They would become bored or fail to

learn something new. Better players may also tend to ease up with less skilled opposition. When this happens, their skills do not improve. Then too, a match is not much fun if the opposition makes so many errors that rallies are short or non-existent.

2. If you want to play socially you'll have to ask people and do the advance work to organize games. This is because of the facts explained above. It has nothing to do with your personality or worth as a person.

3. Learn *The Code* and the *U.S.T.A. Rules* as soon as possible. Through sheer ignorance, players often make mistakes which annoy others or even make others think those players are cheating. It is easier to avoid a bad impression than to correct one later.

4. Don't compare yourself with others in rating your skills, but do assess your own progress. Are you improving? If you don't know, you are setting yourself up for false comparisons with others. Or maybe you are totally complacent. Keep some accurate records and you'll soon know for a fact that you are getting better.

5. Read and remember the *Tennis Etiquette* section in this book.

New Team Players

Maybe you have played tennis for awhile, but you have never been on a team before. Please realize that your needs are secondary to the team's needs. Every year some team members will play positions they don't like and/or have partners they don't want. There is no way around this home truth. Some days, months or years you will be one of them if you're on a team.

Veteran Team Players on a New Team

1. Learn the customs of this new tribe. In other words, learn their rules for practices, absences, etc.

2. Ask lots of questions, preferably before you join, regarding things like lineup position, partnerships and how often you will play.

3. If you had problems on your previous team, analyze what they were and make a plan to avoid repeating them. Ask others if you don't know what the problem was. If you do not accurately diagnose the cause of your previous problems, you are likely to repeat them.

4. Refrain from telling your new team members how much better your old team used to do things.

CHAPTER 23:
Tennis Etiquette

How are we supposed to learn tennis etiquette? Most of us learned the hard way, by making mistakes. Sometimes an experienced player told us what to do. Here are the common rules of tennis etiquette. Most of them have not been written down before. They are passed on from person to person like tribal lore.

1. Honor your commitment to each event. If you are a team member, do not commit yourself to any other activity (tournament, medical appointment, etc.) which takes place at the same time as a team match, even if you are not formally scheduled to play in that particular team match.

   Your team may have an enormous roster, but there's always a possibility you'll be needed. If your team forfeits a point, your teammates will not forget who let them down. Suppose, on the other hand, you cancel your non-team engagement to rush off as an emergency sub for your team match. Then you inconvenience whoever you had an appointment with and that person will be annoyed.

   There is an exception to the above rule. A person who has a prior commitment for certain match or practice days may want to join a team. She should report this commitment to the captain before she joins and ask if the team still wants her, knowing she will not be available on those dates. If they do want her despite her restrictions, she may feel free to join.

2. Don't walk across other courts while they are in play.

3. Don't walk behind players on other courts during play.

4. Don't chase your stray ball on to neighboring courts during play; wait for the players to see the ball and return it to you.

5. Don't drop balls which are not in play on the court during play.

6. Don't drop your second ball behind you after serving. Both #5 and this action may cause a let call, loss of a point or an accident.

7. Don't talk to clinic participants while the tennis pro is talking. Maybe you are not interested, but others have invested in the clinic and may want to recoup their investment.

8. When you are a spectator at matches, don't clap when someone makes an error.

9. Don't delay everyone with interminable breaks for rest, drinks, smoking, chitchat, changes of gear, etc. This is called stalling and it is a violation of *The Code*.

10. Don't return a serve you know is bad; if you do so inadvertently, apologize.

11. If you can't keep a commitment to play in a social match, do your best to find your own replacement.
12. If you are near the net, pass balls directly to your opponents across the net; don't drop them on the ground for players to scramble after. Never smash balls directly at your opponents as a way of returning balls between points. Make an honest attempt to return the balls reasonably close to the server.
13. Balls may rest at the fence on your side when a side change occurs. Pick the balls up and hand them to your opponents at the net.
14. If you cannot play a full length social match because of another commitment, decline the invitation. It is as rude to ruin a match for others by leaving early as it is to arrive late.
15. When you lose a match to less skilled opponents, be gracious. Do not minimize their achievement by reporting on your ailments, lack of practice, etc.
16. Memorize *The Code's* directive for making line calls. If you are not positive about a ball, call it good. Failure to do so constitutes cheating. Playing points over again for these cases is not a kindness and will definitely anger your opponents.
17. Some people like to play tennis in quiet surroundings. Try not to create excessive noise when you play near others.
18. Please call the score out loud before you serve. Tennis is not a quiz game called Guess the Score. Frequent debates and arguments over the score detract from fun.
19. Don't use social tennis as an excuse to break USTA rules and *The Code*, unless everybody agrees to make up their own rules in advance.

Chapter 24:
Tennis Safety

1. Don't catch a bad serve. You might end up with Mallet Finger, a torn tendon of the end of the finger which causes it to droop.
2. Wear plastic lenses in your sunglasses.
3. Take the time to pick up stray balls. It's easy to strain, sprain or break human limbs.
4. Don't play on a wet hard court.
5. Don't play on a soft court with patches of slimy, slippery algae.
6. Use sunblocks faithfully to prevent sunburn, skin cancer and the much dreaded leather hide.
7. Cover your head if you are fair; scalps can burn too.
8. Carry basic first aid supplies with you.
9. Team loyalty does not include aggravating an injury by playing on it.
10. Ice an injury as soon as possible.

PART SIX:
Good Match, Ladies

Warming up for a home match one day we observe the visiting team's arrival. Are their team members striding ahead cheerfully, eager for action? Or are they straggling in with heads down, frowns locked in place? Which kind of team would you rather be on?

A well run team is a joy to be part of. Its matches, meetings, practices and clinics run smoothly. It's members have fun together. They help each other get better and do not compete with each other. Some think such teams occur by miraculous good fortune. The truth is quite different.

By the time you finish *Tasteful Tennis*, you know we believe in organization. You may find the tasks of organizing seem overwhelming. Some tasks like making lineups and partnerships can't be avoided. Some others, like making rules and running meetings can be. You may be tempted to take shortcuts.

Please, don't do it! Through league contacts, through conversations with captains in other cities and through our own team experiences, we have learned what happens to teams who use shortcuts. For a while they seem to run smoothly. Little by little, however, they begin to crumble. Bad feelings escalate and spread. Sometimes tension reaches such a level that the team can't reorganize when they make a valiant effort. They have to break apart completely.

Leaving that dismal picture behind as a warning, we urge you to get your team organized. The process of organizing will draw your members together. And when you're finished, you'll be free to have a great time.

*B*IBLIOGRAPHY

Many of these books can be ordered from the United States Tennis Association. If you join this organization you will also be entitled to a 10% discount on books and supplies, *Tennis USA* plus a subscription to *Tennis* magazine. For an up-to-date list of their offerings or to order any book saying USTA in the listings here contact Publications Dept., USTA, 707 Alexander Rd., Princeton, NJ 08540.

Doubles:

1 Heldman, Gladys M., "The 10 Commandments of Doubles," *World Tennis*, August, 1989, pages 32-35.

Basic Reference:

2 Blue, Clifford. *Tennis Disputes.* 2nd ed., Andover, Mass.: Linesmen Press, 1982. USTA. It settles major controversies you can't find answers for in the *USTA Rules* and *The Code.* The captain should carry a copy to every match to settle disputes in a hurry.

3 Powel, Colonel Nick. *The Code.* USTA. Carry at all times!

4 *Rules of Tennis and Cases and Decisions.* USTA. Carry at all times!

How To:

5. Blaskower, Pat and Joanne Williams. *Women's Winning Doubles.* Santa Barbara Press, 1985. USTA. If you can only order one book in addition to the Basic Reference books, make this the one. It has invaluable information on strategy and psychology for the over 35 woman in an easily understood form.

Inspirational Models:

6 King, Billie Jean and Frank Deford. *Billie Jean.* New York: Viking, 1982. Reveals the human side of a great champion.

7   King, Billie Jean and Kim Chapin. *Billie Jean*. New York: Harper & Row, 1974. What made her run.

8   Gibson, Althea. *I Always Wanted To Be Somebody*. New York: Harper & Row, 1958. Truly inspiring.

Psychology/Motivation:

9   Gallwey, W. Timothy. *Inner Tennis*. New York: Random House, 1976.

10   Geist, Harold and Cecelia Martinez. *Tennis Psychology*. Chicago: Nelson-Hall, 1976.

11   Kriese, Chuck. *Total Tennis Training*. Grand Rapids, Michigan: Masters Press, 1988. USTA.

12   Bunker, Linda and Robert J. Rotella. *Mind, Set & Match*. Englewood Cliffs, N.J.: Prentice-Hall, 1982.

Organization:

13   Brown, Jim. *Tennis: Teaching, Coaching and Directing Programs*. Englewood Cliffs, N.J.: Prentice-Hall Inc., 1976.

14   *Challenge Ladders Information Sheet*. USTA. All you need on one sheet for less than a dollar.

15   *The National Tennis Rating Program Kit*. USTA. Complete guide to the National Tennis Rating Program used by the Volvo and many other leagues.

16   Owens, Eleanor Boland. Tennis: *Easy On-Easy Off*. 1975. USTA. Has round-robin charts you'll need for team practices.

17   Kelly, Julie and Nancy Kirwan. *The Tennis League Handbook*. Finn Hall Enterprises, 1975. USTA. Tells you all you need to know to start an entirely new league.

18   Kraft, Eve and John Conroy. *The Tennis Teacher's Guide: Group Instruction and Team Coaching*. Revised edition, 1989. USTA. Has lots of drills.

Counsel Index